drink london

architecture and alcohol

•••

juanita cheung
photographs by keith collie

drink london

architecture and alcohol

• • • ellipsis

•••

All rights reserved. No part of this publication may be reproduced in any form without written permission from the publisher

BRITISH LIBRARY CATALOGUING IN PUBLICATION
A CIP record for this book is available from the British Library

PUBLISHED BY •••ellipsis
2 Rufus Street London N1 6PE
EMAIL ...@ellipsis.co.uk
WWW http://www.ellipsis.com
SERIES EDITOR Tom Neville
SERIES DESIGN Jonathan Moberly

COPYRIGHT © 2000 Ellipsis London Limited
ISBN 1 899858 76 8

FILM PROCESSING METRO IMAGING

PRINTING AND BINDING Hong Kong

•••ellipsis is a trademark of Ellipsis London Limited

For a copy of the Ellipsis catalogue or information on special quantity orders of Ellipsis books please contact our sales manager on 020 7739 3157 or sales@ellipsis.co.uk

Juanita Cheung 2000

contents

Introduction

So they say London's swinging again ... but where? What does it look like, how is it done, what does it mean? The bars of London play host every night – which sometimes starts at mid-day – to the capital's down-time, that elastic chunk of time between work and home, where one can forget, relax, come alive, get excited, gripe, feel good, meet friends and beautiful strangers, drink, drink and drink some more, be merry, have a brawl but also search for affirmation as to what it is about this city that makes us want it or need it so. Because this is it. It's not the cramped domestic spaces, the hellish rage-filled journeys on its streets and underground or the long competitive work hours that attract. It's the city's playgrounds we're after; it's where we go in pursuit of the act the dictionary describes as 'to be lively and modern'. We put up with the rest in the secure knowledge that it's all happening in our bars. Dr Johnson proclaimed that 'a tavern chair was the throne of human felicity', and right now the best tavern chairs are in London.

The design of where we play is crucial. Some bars give better than others. The local will always do but often we choose bars not out of proximity but rather because the look and feel of a particular space mirrors the public image we have of ourselves. Of course we also go in search of the artful cocktail but more tellingly we also go where they may only serve a few bottled beers. The draw of such a place lies primarily in its design, the atmosphere it engenders and the people it attracts. We might want to live in Mayfair, Notting Hill or Hoxton but we often don't. We might not be able to choose where we live and work or even the people we hang around with but we can choose where we drink.

To like where you drink is a given which does have a down side. 'You chose this place? But why?' Defending it is like defending yourself. Where you drink defines your very being.

> The history of London is a history of its taverns; to know one is to know the other.
> Anon.

The emergence of London's 'style bars' in the last few years is a radical departure in the long history of alcoholic architecture. It developed from a reaction against the lack of variety in existing establishments – mainly pubs and private drinking clubs. The loosening of licensing laws, which basically meant drinking venues could stay open all day, has resulted in the creation of a new type of public space by architects and designers. Apparently it came from the north, Manchester to be precise, which did not suffer the intermediary run of dodgy-looking wine bars experienced by London and other cities. Now, every seven minutes a new bar opens in London … or so it seems. This almost delirious churning out of alcoholic space, more often than not from old garages or banking halls, has no obvious abatement in sight and, judging by their success, the drinking public is insatiable. Not since the gin palaces and ale-houses (licensed to sell only ale or stout which the government promoted to combat the evil effects of gin) of the last century has there been such a marked change in the venues and habits of recreational drinking. While the pubs of London will always have their traditional charm and continue to please many (and, most of all, tourists), these new bars now provide not only a viable alternative, but they are making a significant and lasting impact on the geography of London, being ever-present as both front runners and mainstays of any burgeoning new area. Where the new bars open others seem to follow.

Unsurprisingly, distinctive trends are already beginning to emerge in the design of these bars. The importance of their design, however, rests not with any grandiose notion of architecture. They are not the monuments of our civilisation, they do not purport to be our pyramids or temples (the worshipful adoration of the contents of a bottle does not count); they do not commemorate the power, wealth or taste of a ruling class, nor are they a result of a serious utopian essay. The significance of bar design lies in the unusual combination of high visibility and public experiment.

The design of bars can be seen as the sketches which precede a masterpiece. The lack of heavy-handed legislation behind these minor *chef-d'oeuvres* allows more room for tentative concepts or prototypical design. Together they form a sketchbook from which greater ideas can spring and mature. There is also a certain levity inherent in a bar-design brief which is conducive to playful experimentation. Adolf Loos wrote that an architect 'senses the effect that he wishes to exert on the spectator ... piety if a tomb, homeyness if a residence, gaiety if a tavern'. These relatively small projects with generally decent budgets and relatively few planning constraints have been a welcome vehicle for design innovation.

Another notable advantage in these projects is that this is a fashionable, rapidly consumable architecture that does not necessarily need to last, not literally anyway. It is perhaps more important for the design of a bar to make a lasting impression than to continue unchanged over several years. Just as pop songs do not have to stay in the charts forever, but they do strive to be in the top ten ... bars aim to glow brightly but not eternally. The emphasis is definitely on capturing the present atmosphere, no matter how ephemeral or transient that may be.

And because they are often interior designs, not everyone in the neighbourhood has to approve. They do not strive to be loved by one and all. Technically, each bar must only aim to please enough people to fill it.

This book is a personal selection of bars of architectural significance. It is not a hit list of the most stylish, the most elegant or the most anything, but rather a mixture of types, with a few eccentrics thrown in, and even some outstanding examples of ugliness. In their concepts, forms and details, you will find notable signature styles and the seeds of a greater architectural import. All are worth a drink in as there is no good without evil, and together they form part of the overall picture of *drink london*, a catalogue of the dimly lit, hazily perceived world of architecture and alcohol.

This is primarily an exploration of new spaces, some whose popularity is bewildering and perhaps depressing, and some whose ephemeral beauty may not last more than a few months. As a result of the time that elapses between writing and publication, many new bars will have opened which may supersede the examples included here.There are also drinking venues which are wholly enjoyable yet of little architectural significance which have been omitted: Claridges' bar, basically a reproduction from the 1930s; and such places as the Notting Hill Arts Club, Doghouse, Bug Bar or 291, which may be significant on the bar scene but of little original architectural import. 291 in particular is an interesting space to drink in; there is something deliciously sinister about getting plastered in a church but the added fixtures which make it a bar are ugly and mundane.The large and boisterous Titanic is also omitted since its hype, which you will surely have heard, covers all that is significant about it.

Of course, at present there is a regrettable trend in bar design, significant in number only, which must be acknowledged – the emergence of the new chain-pubs. Frighteningly, interiors of pale walls, pale wood floors, and pale imagination are sprouting up on every corner of the capital, completely disregarding local or any other character. The insulting thing is that they are often marketed as catering to women as if the female drinking population was somehow deficient in design sensibility. Minimalism has been sabotaged and equated with cheapness and the dumbing down of design. The same design strategy seems to have been applied in the super-duper drinking-and-dining emporia such as Mezzo, with the distinction that multiple zeros have been added to the budget. These places will always appeal to the sheep mentality of certain punters – '600 other reasonably well-off people can't be wrong' – and rely on vapid – 'the drinks are expensive therefore I'm expensive' – reasoning for their popularity. They fail to challenge or engage and are depressing both in their dullness and as missed opportunities.

Another unavoidable trend is the theme bar – not a fundamentally evil concept but a recurrent irritant on the bar scene. Unsubtle formulaic design is often shoved down the punter's throat, but this is a democratic world where everyone can vote with their legless drinking feet. In a way it is no worse than the unbridled use of the flea-ridden leather sofa, often in the name of some vacuous *Ellepaper** aesthetic erroneously dubbed 'lounge' which induces an initial personal rage followed by a chuckle: after all it still is someone's 'throne of felicity', just not mine. One can always leave, after a drink, just as Bukowski left his Bar Zero, because the next place is bound to be sweeter.

ACKNOWLEDGEMENTS
I'd like to thank my trusty drinking companions Kim Pryde and Peter Culley for accompanying me on my research trips, and Samantha Meah, Wah and Malu Halasa for their continuing support and encouragement.
JC September 1999

soho

Sak

The plain matt-black street frontage, discreet logo and obscured glass doors conspire to give an air of exclusivity. A single thin strip of clear glass runs across both doors just above eye-level, cleverly making the inside seem more tempting. The next set of double glass doors is acid-etched to leave a floral pattern which looks too pretty.

Inside, the small double-decker space is dominated and flattered by the coloured lighting – yellow back-lit shelves behind the bar, the glowing red of the tiny dining area at the back seen through the water-curtain wall and the double-height lavender lightbox of the stairwell. Furniture by Rock Galpin's Studio Orange is low, inviting and looks as if it would be sweet if tasted. The sofas are like choc-ices with a panel of chocolate licked off the end and the coffee tables have a smooth white layer which looks like icing with a fruity red flavour downstairs to go with the mint-coloured walls. It is mainly a low-key space throughout – decorated by a changing display of inoffensive modern artwork – except for the dramatic over-the-top terrazzo sink in the loos in an unfortunate shade of salmon.

ADDRESS 49 Greek Street, London W1 (020 7439 4159)
CLIENT Mafiosi Ltd (James Roccelli)
UNDERGROUND Leicester Square, Tottenham Court Road
OPEN Monday to Tuesday, 11.30–2.00; Wednesday to Friday, 11.30–3.00; Saturday, 17.30–3.00

Cube 3 1998

Little Italy

Continentally stylish – in a good way. This is hardly groundbreaking design but there is a certain elegance to it, which seems original. Narrow double glass doors appear forever open despite the un-Mediterranean climate. Polished bright-green terrazzo tiles with pebble-size white aggregate give a satisfying sound if adult shoes are worn. It is a slender space with a single row of matching chairs and tables. These are in a milk-chocolate brown wood with off-white steel legs and the seats have a little wavy, ruffly bit as if a little Italian flair could not be contained. A glass-topped, lit ledge shaped like the figure 7 aids those balancing on their own limbs. Opposite, the bar is a thick Barolo red marble slab perched on a sliver of lit glass above a matt stainless-steel front. There is a double-decker restaurant area at the back and one can easily see, smell and relish both floors of heavenly garlic and olive-oil feasts.

Owned by the Bar Italia people, this bar could have gone all-out to capitalise on a ready-made loyal clientele but the mood here is decidedly different and appeals to a crowd which, if not older, is more sophisticated and notably paunchier.

ADDRESS 21 Frith Street, London W1 (020 7734 4737)
CLIENT the Poledri family and Claudio Camera
UNDERGROUND Piccadilly Circus, Tottenham Court Road
OPEN Monday to Saturday, 12.00–3.00; Sunday, 12.00–22.30

Peter Davidson 1997

Little Italy

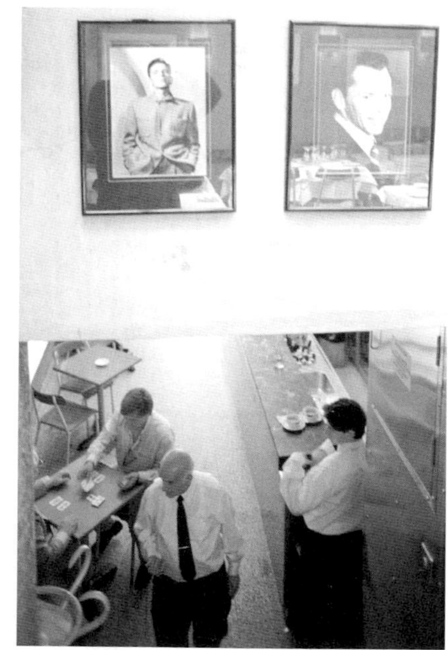

soho

Peter Davidson 1997

Tactical

A scruffy split-personality bar which triumphantly defies the vulgar Mezzo-isation of Soho. Its cold steel and harsh concrete finishes – like an out-of-character act of toughness – do not mask a genuinely relaxed and comfortable atmosphere and Tactical is the perfect domain for the perpetually freelance.

This lovable little drinking den has been created by linking two shopfronts into a Siamese-twinned space. The furniture is a mixture: stock grey plastic chairs and wooden tables with plié-ing aluminium legs on one side and aluminium tables with wooden plié-ing legs on the other. Cages of books, journals and fanzines which can be bought earlier in the day act as backdrop to the various activities which have been known to take place here. Although impromptu poetry happenings may sound a bit too black-polo-necked and wheatgrassy, these evenings lack any ambitious aggression and are relatively few and far between, leaving only harmless remnants such as the white markings on the floor (a study of the movement patterns of the space). A hybrid collage whose rough seams will hopefully survive long after flashier Soho has run its course.

ADDRESS 26–27 D'Arblay Street, London W1 (020 7287 2823)
CLIENT Astrid Skelly
UNDERGROUND Oxford Circus
OPEN Monday to Friday, 9.00–23.00; Saturday, 12.00–23.00; Sunday 12.00–22.30 (happy hour 17.00–19.00)

Alan Houston 1997

Alan Houston 1997

Candy Bar

Formerly called Fred's, this place is significant as a pioneer in contemporary bar design. The tiny shop front on Carlisle Street opened as a members' bar catering to local media types but was surprisingly friendly and laid-back during off-peak times. Back in the mid-1980s, the frosted glass screen of the entrance which hid a tiny raised seating area, the industrial-looking steel spiral staircase, and the bendy steel tentacle bar lights looked strikingly new and different to the other drinking dens of Soho. Bar snacks were a relatively new concept and served in tiny glass bowls and the menus were intimidatingly cool-looking in aluminium. This all sounds shockingly mediocre now but it did pave the way for non-pub, non-gentlemen's-club drinking venues which were scarce back then. The three floors are still jam-packed with suits but they are all worn by women as it is now a lesbian bar with a men-as-guests-only door policy.

ADDRESS 4 Carlisle Street, London W1 (020 7494 4041)
CLIENT Fred Taylor
UNDERGROUND Tottenham Court Road
OPEN Monday to Thursday, 17.00–24.00; Friday, 17.00–2.00; Saturday, 14.00–2.00; Sunday, 17.00–23.00

Chassay Wright Architects 1987

Freedom

1.10 When this bar first opened it was a gay young thing. Clean and cool, it felt like a modern gallery space with clients as exhibits. The whiteness of the walls and the unadorned openness of the then still somewhat rare large plate-glass-window front had the stark crispness of a fresh white cotton T-shirt. There were unresolved bits like the awkward shape of the blocks which were the loos but on the whole the design felt appropriate and current. Time has unfortunately not been kind. Neither has the last refurbishment. A raised platform has been added, creating the clutter of a step up and a handrail with large orange and yellow lit circles. The dingy blue Dalsouple flooring also has plate-size purple circles in it and in fact there are circles everywhere – in the high-backed stingy-in-depth booth seats, blue and yellow ones around the perimeter of the room and cut-out ones in the chairs. A segment of the wall has been mysteriously panelled in red and purple padded velvet. Someone obviously thought they would groovy up the place. Its one beauty now is the space by the window which unfolds to allow those near it front-row seats for – and at spitting distance from – the Wardour Street people parade and the fragrant fumes of Soho nights.

ADDRESS 60–66 Wardour Street, London W1 (020 7734 0071)
CLIENT Robert Newmart
UNDERGROUND Piccadilly Circus
OPEN Monday to Saturday, 11.00–3.00; Sunday, 11.00–23.00

Mark Langthorne 1994; refurbished by Robert Newark 1997

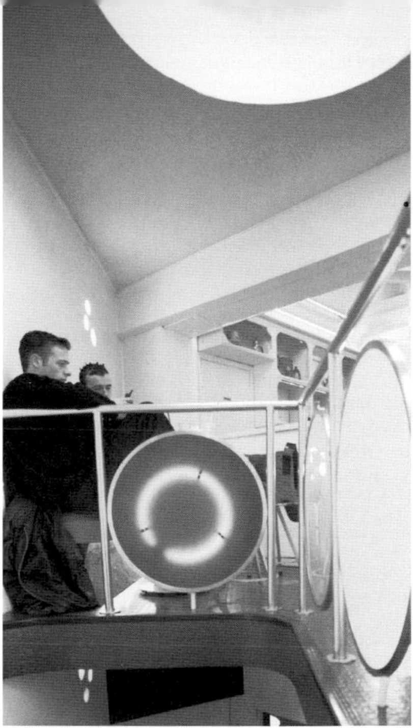

soho

Mark Langthorne 1994; refurbished by Robert Newark 1997

Lab

The colour and form of the bright stripes on the window are reminiscent of the graphics popular during the Charlie's Angels' years. Images of patches sewn on to denim and Snoopy during his more elongated period in the 1970s drift through the mind. The interior colour scheme is another walk down Memory Lane – brick walls painted avocado green are matched with a bronze orangey-brown, the exact colour of Farrah Fawcett's tan. A protruding rounded capsule form with curved wooden edges is the repeated theme as it gives form to the bar front, the lit shelves fixed behind the bar and around the room, and the mirror frames. A similar structure is used for the hinged bar-height tables on the ground floor which actually look like mini versions of the built-into-the-wall pull-down beds also from the 1970s.

Downstairs, purple loo doors have more globular built-up shapes surrounding their honeycomb fly-eyed windows and are cheekily marked 'bitches' and 'bastards'. Other details include silver curved-wedge amplifiers and circular lightboxes by the stairs which have images composed of little square boxes of colour as used on incognito television interviewees. Squint and they are ... small flames? No, the answer is pornographic – just a nice bit of contextual site history.

ADDRESS 12 Old Compton Street, London W1 (020 7437 7820)
UNDERGROUND Leicester Square, Tottenham Court Road
OPEN Monday to Saturday, 10.00–24.00; Sunday, 17.00–23.00

Paul Daly 1999

Lab

soho

Paul Daly 1999

The Player

1.14 This members' bar owes its seedy glamour as much to its location below the fluffy kitten-heeled purveyor of fine undergarments, Agent Provocateur, as to its decor. Self-billed as a jet-set airport cocktail lounge, it has inadvertently drawn attention to the fact that its design is about as sexy as a complimentary pair of in-flight nylon socks. Executive departure lounges are still, on the whole, rather dull corporate affairs meant to appeal to those who think city boardrooms are the epitome of style, and hardly the thing to aspire to in a Soho drinking den. This bar is in fact a clean, comfortable place where you could happily take your grandmother. Low, rounded baby-buggy-shaped, blue leather seats are spread across the 'P' logo-ed carpet which looks like the enlarged pattern of a 1970s dad's tie. Matching booth seats snake around the orangey-pink walls to which a subtle sprinkling of glitter has been added. Hidden lights behind the back booth seats project pleasing fan-patterned illuminations on the wall. Pleasant but hardly daring.

ADDRESS 8–12 Broadwick Street, London W1 (020 7494 9125)
UNDERGROUND Tottenham Court Road
OPEN Monday to Sunday, 17.00–23.00

Gordon Thompson 1998

The Player

Gordon Thompson 1998

Alphabet

A couple of years ago this was one of the key players in part of a move westwards from the more rambunctious parts of Soho (a move which luckily has not destroyed the area for the odd pedestrian who still wants to use the pavement for walking rather than standing around in impossibly tight formations outside pubs). Alphabet is composed of a surprisingly amply proportioned ground-floor room and a basement, unusual for being neither subterranean and cavernous nor teeny-tiny with a Napoleon complex like some of its neighbours.

From the outside, Alphabet looks like an ad agency's reception area during a media event, especially when it's full, with the bar obscured. The gutted space has wisely been left relatively simple with minimal intervention. The use of bare concrete borders on the overwhelming. Most chairs and tables are a mixture of boxy nondescript new and second-hand pieces. Downstairs, however, chairs have been greatly influenced by an early 1980s Ron Arad Rover recipe (which incidentally used Jean Prouvé's early 1920s chairs as more than just an influence). If these should look dated and annoy, be grateful that this was furnished in pre-salvaged-leather-sofa days. The tightly packed fibre-optic cables which decorate the side of the stairs will have you wondering, 'Is it Art?' Cleverness in bar-name interpretation can be found in the blown-up graphics of an A–Z map page transferred on to the surface of the floor. Upstairs a series of moodily painted objects – 26, to be precise – can entertain the eye and mind and become the focus should conversation become a bit stilted.

ADDRESS 61–63 Beak Street, London W1 (020 7439 2190)
CLIENTS Spike Marchant
UNDERGROUND Oxford Circus
OPEN Monday to Friday, 12.00–23.00; Saturday, 16.00–23.00

Jenny Jones 1997

Jenny Jones 1997

Circus

Minimal. Screen-printed green glass panels hide stairwell down. Singular steel-tube handrail. Bottom of stairs, large dark-wood door. Cool blue-white glow emanating from bar – three sides of square space. Fourth side steps down to longer space. Square bed, table, bed, table. Row of soft single seats on right. Row of deep square detail-less windows on left. Cream fabric, dark wood, black opaque glass. White gravel, bamboo outside. Should serve only neat drinks.

ADDRESS 1 Upper James Street, London W1 (020 7534 4000)
CLIENT Mirror Image Restaurants plc
UNDERGROUND Piccadilly Circus
OPEN Monday to Friday, 12.00–15.00, 18.00–24.00; Saturday, 18.00–24.00

David Chipperfield Architects 1997

Circus

soho

David Chipperfield Architects 1997

Gold Bar Café

A few decades on – or more than likely just one – there will be a 1990s revival signalled by the use of lightboxes everywhere. Habitat will sell do-it-yourself kits and we'll reminisce about how the original ones were ubiquitous, swinging and cool.

The images of the lightboxes used here were created by photographer Tim Brotherton and artist/graphic designer Christian Soukias who responded to the brief calling for a diptych of lightboxes – one placed at the front of the bar and one at the back – in order to lead the eye (and, more importantly, the drinking parts of the face) into the bar. The images are of the inside of a fridge and then of another fridge – unrecognisable as a glowing rectangular object powered by a generator in the middle of a field. The thing about lightboxes is that one tends to look at the aggressively bright display of colours and patterns and avoid taking in any contextual meaning of the image displayed. Whatever is depicted looks like pop art. The mundane subject is immediately imbued with a sense of irony – though the what and whys are never made clear, leaving the viewer no wiser.

There is actually a lot more going on in this tiny space. It avoids feeling as cramped as it might, perhaps because the whole façade can be opened up and the pedestrianised area immediately in front can be visually appropriated, giving a false sense of spaciousness.

The colours of the walls, Melamine tables (on chrome bases), Robin Day stools, vinyl upholstering to the bar stools and seat backing are a mix 'n' match selection of light blues, browns and reds. The flooring has the same colour and texture as rubber bands. Everything is extra small and the lack of precision in detailed craftsmanship – of the upholstered corners, for example – is excusable in the same way that on close inspection Barbie's clothes never really fit or look that well made – it

Hudson Featherstone 1999

Gold Bar Café

Hudson Featherstone 1999

is not expected of teeny-tiny things.

Overall, Gold Bar has a 1970s leisure-suit aesthetic which calls for a high-tech fabric name – Crimplene, Dacron, or perhaps Elast-o-bar. The bar design seems quite unselfconscious until you focus on the row of Verner Panton pendant lights hanging over the walnut Formica bar top. Other heavily designer-conscious details successfully stop the bar from appearing too retro. These include a mirror with sand-blasted circular light cut-outs and variously sized round glass blocks embedded in the recast strip of concrete flooring at the front which let a bit of daylight into the basement area. The narrow stairs which lead to the lower ground floor glow a bright orange and the handrail is lit with flickering lights. One would expect the cumulative effect of these many parts to result in confusion but instead it is a pleasant example of that cliché of a little space with a lot of personality.

ADDRESS 23a Ganton Street, London W1 (020 7434 0109)
UNDERGROUND Oxford Circus
OPEN Monday to Saturday 11.00–23.00

Gold Bar Café

Hudson Featherstone 1999

Two Floors

This bar had a lived in, loved in, run-down feel to it the moment it opened. Misinterpreting this as 'a look' whose formula could be obtained and copied, many other places have since opened with the correct props arranged just so – but these on the whole remain spiritless and unimpressive. Two Floors is an original whose success may be difficult to pinpoint.

It's not the furniture. This is commonplace and not all that exciting. The orange, grey and white steel IKEA stools have been replaced by the kind of moulded, light-coloured plywood seats used to kit out mundane conference halls. Beat-up old grungy leather sofas are miles past their last legs but they fit the space and don't look as if they want to budge. For some reason, perhaps because they were among the first to infiltrate a London bar, these do not irritate as other examples do. Would it be reading too much into the sofa's aura to imagine that *this* one was bought after someone became infatuated with it and wanted to give it a home? The rest of the fixtures – a steel-fronted, wooden-topped bar, funky paint colours and a few banquettes downstairs – are also unremarkable.

Perhaps it is the unobtrusiveness of the decor which does not try aggressively to upstage its occupants. They probably wouldn't rise to it anyway. Even its name is unaspiringly descriptive, in contrast to others such as 'Fantasy Bar' or 'Home'. It is a lovable place which only annoys during its more popular moments when it tends to be on the crowded side – but its real friends will sit these out.

Most likely it is not the things found in the space which constitute the appeal but the space itself and its location. With high ceilings and large windows at either end, it feels open and hospitable. It relies on the use of its relationship to both street and alleyway as backdrop and focal point. The alleyway in particular is as crucial as it is fascinating, as much of 'close-up London' is. The din of Piccadilly Circus is seconds away, but

Andreas Akerlund and Patric Franzen 1995

Two Floors

Andreas Akerlund and Patric Franzen 1995

it is intriguingly peaceful. It is as if things have temporarily stopped in order for one to scrutinise the details not only of the opposing façades but also of the steel fire escape, an enclosing chain, rubbish bins and the bar's own perforated roll-down shutters. The atmosphere of this bar feeds off their urban charm and makes one feel strangely good about the city one has chosen to drink in.

ADDRESS 3 Kingly Street, London W1 (020 7439 1007)
CLIENT Andreas Akerlund
UNDERGROUND Piccadilly Circus, Oxford Circus
OPEN Monday to Saturday, 10.00–23.00

Two Floors

soho

Andreas Åkerlund and Patric Franzen 1995

YO! Below

Below YO! ... Sushi is where you will find this Japanese beer hall and sake cellar which finally opened in summer 1999, just as interest in the YO!-above empire was starting to wane.

The most significant aspect of this design is the downward shift in eye-level which is emphasised by the angle at which you approach the space as you descend via the industrial steel-grilled fire-escape-like stairs. A cool purplish-blue glows off the white-painted walls and there is a slight feeling of apprehension as you gingerly step into the subterranean expanse – have you just stepped on to a floor, bench or table?

The raised (or lowered, depending how you look at it) seating takes up half the space and cut-out holes have tables of the same pale wood bridging across. Thin circular cushions are provided for comfort. Long bar tops line the opposite corner where once again a double-take is necessary to check the levels as bar staff look deceptively short of leg. Forgive them their awkward dimensions as they will provide five different types of hot and cold sake as well as a special selection of sake-based cocktails. Some of the Alvar Aalto rip-off stools have cut-off legs which impart a kindergarten cuteness to them. The left-over space is a dance-floor but if you are at all self-conscious about your moves decline politely as the seated drinkers have a view which is not pretty – people look like top-heavy lumbering giants.

The bottom-lit tables intensify the which-way-is-up feeling. An aluminium strip in the centre has a self-serve beer pump – apparently YO! Below has the only available licence – which, at the push of a button, gives exactly a third of a pint of Kirin beer, which then registers on a meter by the side of the table. This is addictive fun although you do feel a bit like a hamster pushing for pellets in a laboratory cage – 'drinking in the name of science'. Glowing recessed ashtrays are fitted with special smoke-

Simon Conder Architects and Simon Woodroffe 1999

Simon Conder Architects and Simon Woodroffe 1999

extractors and when you tire of the gadgetry, sit back and enjoy the Manga cartoons playing on the recessed TVs or summon up a Kao (Tranquility), Kubi Kapa (Heaven's Gate) or Te (Tenderness) massage – available free on request.

ADDRESS 52 Poland Street, London W1 (020 7437 0500)
CLIENT Simon Woodroffe
UNDERGROUND Oxford Circus
OPEN Monday to Sunday, 12.00–23.00

Simon Conder Architects and Simon Woodroffe 1999

YO! Below

Simon Conder Architects and Simon Woodroffe 1999

west end

Point 101

On its completion in 1966, and even before he'd seen the T-shirts, the architect Erno Goldfinger described Richard Seifert's Centre Point as London's first pop-art skyscraper. Notorious for spending the first ten years of its life unoccupied, Centre Point is still one of, if not the most significant post-war buildings in London. This is partly due to its role in introducing the tall speculative office block into Britain but also for its innovative use of pre-cast concrete and for what was referred to in the *New York Times* in 1971 as its 'cartoon modern' style. Though it is now listed, Centre Point continues to fuel controversy but at present it seems to be enjoying an upturn in popularity.

Back in May 1968, *Building* magazine claimed in an article equating the building with the Beatles and Mary Quant that 'More than any other London building, Centre Point makes London swing, it backs Britain'. So it's quite appropriate in this second swinging of London that it now plays host to a bar. In the area once occupied by a branch of the NatWest bank, the glazed ground- and first-floor space sits beneath a 50-metre glass bridge which links the tower with the maisonettes behind. The concept behind the refurbishment stems from its location at a central tube and bus junction and also from its role as a key orientation point. The intention was to create a transit-lounge space where people would meet as they arrive, depart, connect and link. The original fabric has been retained with its glass and marble tiled walls, its Florentine tile floors and the stunning pattern of the white Carrera marble brick shapes with black terrazzo infill which cover the floor where the banking hall used to be.

The new main bar, fronted with horizontal grooves in beech, has been placed under a baby-blue drop ceiling on a slightly skew angle which encourages circulation in and around the seating areas. A selection of Eames chairs and tables (LCW, LCM and DCW) are spread between the two

Stephen Donald 1998

Stephen Donald 1998

floors with new wooden built-in banquettes upstairs arranged in opposing rows to feel like a railway carriage. These give an excellent view of the original external tapered pillars which are now spotlit to counter the shadow from the bridge overhang.

While the old mahogany and galvanised-metal stairs have been retained as an alternative exit, a new double-height stairwell of *in-situ* polished concrete has been added. There is also a massive new sliding door whose familiar chunky form is a reference to the previously mentioned pillars. Above the spiral glass doors there is a huge screen which can been seen both internally and externally. When the bar first opened, a three-minute promotional video – specially commissioned by the Architectural Foundation – was played which showed the space animated by dancing Eames chairs and their fire-extinguisher partners in what must have been a binary-coded homage to the mops and buckets of *Fantasia*.

ADDRESS 101 New Oxford Street, London WC1 (020 7379 3112)
CLIENT The Mean Fiddler
UNDERGROUND Tottenham Court Road
OPEN Monday to Thursday, 11.00–2.00; Friday to Saturday, 11.00–2.30; Sunday, 11.00–23.00

Stephen Donald 1998

Point 101

west end

Stephen Donald 1998

Lobby Bar

As its banal name suggests, this bar is located in the lobby of the Jestico + Whiles-designed One Aldwych hotel.

The building was originally designed in 1907 by the Anglo-French team of Mewes and Davis to house the offices of *The Morning Post* newspaper. Although the interior of the building has been almost entirely gutted, the external façade of Norwegian granite and the Westmoreland-slate mansard roof were kept intact. From the outside the only clues to the building's new occupants are the unusually modern use of rosemary bushes growing in the window sills as a decorative element and the giant silver planters signalling the entrance to something quite keen on making a contemporary design statement. While the façade has been left unchanged, the building has actually been dramatically altered through a fundamental change in its orientation. If entering at the distinctive and original corner entrance, one would quickly be ushered downstairs before even noting the abrupt change in direction. These doors now only serve the Axis bar (see page 2.10) and restaurant, both of which are found below ground.

The entrance to the hotel and Lobby Bar are actually on the side of the building fronting Kingsway. Coming from Aldwych you find yourself U-turning back into the space and looking directly at the bar. As the structure of the building still points to the original main entrance, the bar looks as if it is blocking the exit. Two rows of bottles across the arched, former inner doorway now symbolically bolt one in for another drink. The large empty double-height space and the pale polished-limestone floor give the impression of sudden exposure and one hurries along past the white, minutely fluted pillars to the sanctuary of the darker, carpeted bar area. The bar matches the original dark-oak panelling surrounding the large windows.

Mary Fox Linton/Gordon Campbell Gray 1998

Lobby Bar

Mary Fox Linton/Gordon Campbell Gray 1998

Lobby Bar

The dramatic floral displays which sit in the space – two atop a pair of incredibly high Perspex pillars – are the work of the contemporary florist Stephen Woodhams, whose tiny shop is also in the hotel. These are ever-changing displays and at Easter 1999 featured an incredibly dramatic 'Easter tree' structure of alternating silver-painted pots of daffodils and large Easter eggs.

It's easy to identify with Andre Wallace's copper sculpture. An over-sized boatman sitting in a tiny boat with gigantic oars projects out into the vast height of the space. He too seems to be trying to escape the vulnerability of being in the open by paddling to the side. The two oxidised green paddles pick up the colour of the copper cupola on top of the corner of the building outside. As you turn to leave, you're met with the stare of Emily Woods' stone Dionysus daring you to stay and drink yourself into a bacchanalian stupor.

The furniture in the lobby bar was designed by managing director Gordon Campbell Gray, with the help of interior designer Mary Fox Linton. Before he opened One Aldwych, Gray stayed in five-star hotels around the world, presumably for inspiration. The source for Lobby Bar's high-backed wooden chairs is the Amankila Hotel in Bali. The steel-mesh wall with fibre-optic lighting sounds high tech but actually gives a more relaxed and muted feel to the space than, for instance, a pure stainless-steel wall.

ADDRESS One Aldwych, 1 Aldwych, London WC2 (020 7300 1000)
CLIENT Gordon Campbell Gray
UNDERGROUND Covent Garden, Charing Cross
OPEN Monday to Friday, 9.00–23.00; Saturday and Sunday, 10.00–22.30

Mary Fox Linton/Gordon Campbell Gray 1998

Lobby Bar

Mary Fox Linton/Gordon Campbell Gray 1998

Axis

If you end up here only because you are lost and are really meant to be having a tipple at the Lobby Bar (see page 2.6), never mind – there *is* another bar at the end of this downward-spiralling Alice-in-Wonderland journey. Actually, reach out before the end of the journey or risk falling all the way down to the main dining area of the Axis restaurant where you're really meant to eat too. The rich, liquidly smooth surface of the travertine stairs and walls look like they should feel warm to the touch, as if they were made of toffee instead of stone. The form resembles the inside of a shell and the dizzy, off-balance sensation it produces means that this shell has been tumbling around at the bottom of the ocean.

Inside the semi-circular bar with its Bill Amberg-ed floor, one looks out over and on to the diners below and a huge double-height mural by the English artist Richard Walker entitled 'Amber City'. Reminiscent of the dynamic forms of the Italian Futurists, the spinning vortex of burnt brown, yellow, and orange makes the head continue to spin and momentarily engulfs you in a feeling of disorientation worthy of a Hitchcock dream sequence.

Apparently the name Axis is to do with its location at a point right between the City and the West End. However, it must have something to do with the way everything around you seems to be rotating … and you haven't even had that drink yet.

ADDRESS One Aldwych, 1 Aldwych, London WC2 (020 7300 1000)
CLIENT Gordon Campbell Gray
UNDERGROUND Covent Garden, Charing Cross
OPEN Monday to Friday, 12.00–14.45, 18.00–23.30; Saturday, 18.00–23.30

Mary Fox Linton/Gordon Campbell Gray 1998

Axis

Mary Fox Linton/Gordon Campbell Gray 1998

Cinnamon Bar

Not a real bar as it doesn't serve real drinks. This coffee/juice bar is part of the One Aldwych hotel. A clean, energetic-looking space which has the odd combination of being comfortable but not relaxing. The subdued and simple lighting seems refreshing rather than sleep-inducing after the noisy car-fumed haze of Kingsway. The bar has a brushed-steel front on a shiny base to match the chrome bar-height tables and chairs. The chairs are blue rounded plastic (De Bombo designed by Stefano Giovannoni) – a design which seems to be cropping up everywhere – and the circular tables are packed with cinnamon below their glass surface. The amusing floor tiles are printed with an image of a smooth layer of pebbles. A piece of artwork made of dried cinnamon bark hangs on the end wall. More modern flower arranging from Stephen Woodhams. The espresso machine glows a greenish yellow. A neat place.

ADDRESS One Aldwych, 1 Aldwych, London WC2 (020 7300 1000)
CLIENT Gordon Campbell Gray
UNDERGROUND Aldwych, Holborn
OPEN Monday to Friday, 7.00–21.00; Saturday, 9.00–21.00

Gordon Campbell Gray/Mary Fox Linton 1999

Cinnamon Bar

Gordon Campbell Gray/Mary Fox Linton 1999

Bank

Wipe-clean surfaces and the colours used, together with the din of its many clients' voices give this venue the frenetic ambience of a McDonald's. At £2.50, the famine-sized portion of chips gives the game away, as this is actually a swanky bar and restaurant which caters to work-hard, play-hard suits who prefer to pay more for their bar snacks. Large letters on the glass façade are reminiscent of the prescriptive mottoes usually associated with Kentucky Fried coffee and noodle bars or the early 1990s selling of utilitarian chinos and pocket-Ts. A large multi-panelled mural depicts a Coney Island scene which looks like a jacket for a book about the malaise of a dysfunctional family. The banquettes, bar stools and shiny black wooden chairs are all upholstered in a glossy flame-red leather. There are small tables of varnished MDF and the high wood-panelled bar is topped in a black terrazzo with dark pearly luminescent aggregate. The massive piece of steel which forms the kitchen in the narrow space between bar and restaurant looks not unlike an engine room. Loos are spacious, bright and cheerful in blindingly bright orange, yellow and blue glass-mosaic tiles set in square patterns. The mirrored side wall makes the space look monstrously huge and even changes the landscape of Aldwych outside. Watch cars drive into other cars, or move closer to the window and feel overpowered by the histrionically floodlit Corinthian columns of Bush House opposite. This mirror also successfully highlights the breath-taking expanse of the staggered pieces of green-edged glass which form an illuminated teardrop-shaped plan recess in the ceiling. Hidden spot-lights play refractive games which are hypnotic and sublime.

ADDRESS 1 Kingsway, London WC2 (020 7379 9797)
UNDERGROUND Covent Garden, Holborn
OPEN Monday to Saturday, 11.00–23.00; Sunday, 11.30–21.30

Wickham & Associates Architects 1997

Wickham & Associates Architects 1997

Denim

Why did the ground-breaking, world's first fully glass revolving door go? Because the client wanted a view across to the other side of the road. Rick Mather, architect of the original design of this bar for the restaurant Now and Zen (later renamed WestZenders), sadly noted its passing as he drove by the new bar. The new clients didn't think the doors were conducive to the new bar function and blew them out with explosives. Evidently they thought that having to look through more than one pane of dirty glass would be too much for the clientele and cleaning it regularly would be too much for the staff.

Luckily (or stingily), everything else was kept intact yet the aim was to change it beyond recognition. The glass-bowl water-fountain dragon was apparently removed because *feng shui* was no longer such a great concern. What the client wanted was something quite graphic to reflect a personal fascination with the powerful lines of Manga magazine artwork. Hot, vivid colours were requested and supplied in predominantly dark violets and saturated pinks. Amusingly, the clients balked at the original pink of the padded tiles Velcro-ed to the rear wall, claiming this would make the bar too effeminate and attract the wrong clientele. They were replaced by yellowy-orange ones which were regarded as a safer bet! It would be futile to speculate on where exactly they drew the line on pinkness ...

The most striking element of the new design is the wall of square lightboxes. This is made all the more dramatic by a mirror positioned to look as if the wall were double its length. Sitting in the bar at night, a faded version extends spectacularly over St Martin's Lane. These reflected lightboxes look like the tower-block windows of a cartoon *Metropolis*, certainly more exciting than the reality which is Stringfellows. The lights are machine sequenced and one can look through them to see blurred

Shaun Clarkson 1998

Shaun Clarkson 1998

neon letters which spell 'Denim'. Furniture in the same colours are all soft and boxy. Single goldfish in bachelor-pad glass bowls have matching purple gravel.

Downstairs the vibe is very different and a lot more clubby. The dominant colour is ruby red and the focal point is a baby-blue domed light which protrudes from behind the back of a square sofa. If this really were a cartoon, people would probably line up to place their hands on the dome as in the film *Sleeper* where Woody Allen's robot gets fixated on a feel-good-vibe-dispensing orb. No sign of any jeans though, ring-spun or otherwise.

Tip: if you don't want to risk being turned away – do not dress like Ken Livingstone.

ADDRESS 4a Upper St Martin's Lane, London WC2 (020 7497 0376)
CLIENTS Richard and Antony Travis, Antony Khan
UNDERGROUND Leicester Square
OPEN Monday to Saturday, 12.00–1.00; Sunday, 12.00–22.30

Denim

west end

Shaun Clarkson 1998

The Social

With the opening of this bar, the West End may soon become 'the new Hoxton'. Although Mash, Villandry and R K Stanley can all be found in close proximity, they are spread out over a relatively large area north of Oxford Street. Adjoining streets remain surprisingly quiet in the evenings – with a kind of atmospheric tranquillity verging on the poetic and normally only found in gritty urban novels.

The smoked mirror-lined walls, purple velvet curtains and small tables 'for the girls' of this former strip-joint have been replaced by a sleek, ultra-modern interior with an unusual combination of materials and music no longer restricted to the 'bump-and-grind' variety. The new façade with a large folding shutter of galvanised steel and diffusing glass opens to reveal a long pale corridor clad in vertical and horizontal strips of Eflex, a mix of timber fibres in cement normally used as the external cladding of factories. In fact there are many other examples of external and roofing materials used in this interior which is in keeping with the funny topsy-turvy logic to the design of the space.

Great effort has been used to bring daylight into the lower-ground level – this includes the double-height bar at the front by the entrance and the wide fire escape/lightwell added at the back. Fluorescent lights behind glass-reinforced-plastic panels further dispel any lurking darkness. It's so bright for a basement that one has the strange feeling that it must be hot outside and that the coolness you feel is of the air-conditioned sort. The row of impressively solid-looking exposed concrete booths were cast *in-situ* using timber shuttering and also look as if they were used to provide a cool respite from what must be the sweltering sun outside.

At the same time the ground floor has been totally blocked out and clad in American oak boards (normally used for flooring) which cover all walls and ceiling – with the original Douglas fir floorboards sanded

Adjaye & Russell 1999

The Social

Adjaye & Russell 1999

and sealed to match – leaving the space with a disquieting but not unpleasant feeling of isolation. Actually it is like a sauna, or perhaps an Arctic-Circle shack where an indoor climate has been artificially created and the outdoors is too inhospitable even to warrant a view. Baked-bean-coloured leather is used for the seating with the tables and the simple lighting in black structural steel. The L-shaped light fitting is composed of a tube of fluorescent light beneath which hangs a single light bulb. Each banquette has its own little dimmer switch as a sort of architectural jukebox where customers can select their own atmosphere! The almost Amish approach to simplicity shows a certain fanaticism in the replacement of the normal, admittedly ugly, beer-tap labels with pieces of rectangular aluminium with 'Pilsner' and 'Miller' inscribed in a plain font.

Further wonderfully strange use of materials include the lead urinals, Hexalite – a material normally used for carcassing in the aircraft industry – panelling to the back of the bar downstairs and grey pigmented plaster in the loos which resembles roof slate.

ADDRESS 5 Little Portland Street, London W1 (020 7636 4992)
CLIENTS The Breakfast Group Ltd with Heavenly Recordings
UNDERGROUND Oxford Circus, Tottenham Court Road
OPEN Monday to Saturday, 11.00–24.00; Sunday, 11.00–22.30

Adjaye & Russell 1999

The Social

west end

Adjaye & Russell 1999

Detroit

What can only be described as sand-dune architecture, this subterranean bar looks as if it has been hollowed out of the ground deep below the cobbles of Covent Garden. The sandy texture, however, seems inconsistent with the central London location and feels as if it belongs more to the mythical deserts so often depicted in films and computer games. In fact the walls are made of sand imported from the Adriatic sea, mixed with a resin polymer and applied like everyday plaster.

Originally designed to be a restaurant (Jones) and later converted to the bar Detroit, Quentin Reynolds – who has been involved in several other bar and restaurant projects (including R K Stanley; see page 2.52) – found the various constraints of the site and building regulations actually led to the unconventional design. He thought the awkward angles of the ceiling and non-linearity of the asymmetrical site could be given a certain unity by the curved fluid forms. Indeed, the space does seem to flow seamlessly between what would have been hard-to-read disjointed rooms. Like natural cavernous openings, the unusual layout with changing floor and ceiling heights actually lends a wonderful mystery to the atmosphere. The mere act of finding a seat in this bar brings out feelings of the triumphant excavator – the Howard Carter deeply buried within us all – rising in the noble search for a few seats together and a bit of table space to put down our selection of potions.

Painter/designer Reynolds was searching to create a 'Star Wars bar' atmosphere. Other films which come to mind are *Dune*, *Naked Lunch* and the Mad Max movies. This influence can also be seen in details such as the lighting fixtures. These steel blimps have a series of cut-out holes from which light projects, forming engaging little patterns on the wall. They also have a 1950s sci-fi look to them and indeed the inspiration for these is cited as *Flash Gordon's War of the Worlds*. Other lights glow a

Quentin Reynolds 1995

Detroit

Quentin Reynolds 1995

luminous blue from within cavities in the wall. A predominantly red stained-glass panel and the orange portholes in the doors signify a sort of 1980s film-aesthetic version of the sacred drinking temples of exotic bazaars.

Furniture is a little disappointing – the wood and steel-tube-framed chairs and red and blue banquettes are not as inspired as the space itself. Other details to look out for are the zinc fins dividing the alcoves at the back, the strange purple steps to nowhere (double-click to enter a new world!), the white floating ceiling discs and the clever handrail gouged out of the curved wall. Unfortunately, a slight feeling of unease does creep in just as you are enjoying the sensuous feeling of sliding your hand along inside – the disconcerting feeling is that if you didn't tell the truth you could lose your hand!

ADDRESS 35 Earlham Street, London WC2 (020 7240 2662)
CLIENT Fred Taylor
UNDERGROUND Covent Garden
OPEN Monday to Saturday, 17.00–24.00

Quentin Reynolds 1995

Freedom Brewing Company

The somewhat inaccurately and confusingly named 'Soho Brewing Company' was meant to be a flagship for a chain of American-style microbreweries seeking to be associated with the drinking dens of Soho rather than the shopping centre of Covent Garden. It has since changed its name and a little bit of its image as well. This cavernous space used to have an empty warehouse sparseness to it and while it successfully conveyed the idea of a working brewery, it did not look particularly inviting for extended bouts of drinking. Its hard seating looked uncomfortable and a bit utilitarian, as if you were meant just to have a taster and then lug home a month's supply, possibly at a slightly discounted price.

Maybe the struggle of opening a factory in a listed building, and one in a conservation area with the added complication of the existing attached mall, left the architects little energy or inclination for the leisure part of the brief. They did, however, come back nine months later to make the necessary changes. The almost captivating upside-down textured landscape of exposed services has wisely been left – with the sloped and vaulted ceiling still covered with large aluminium vents, lighting and sound-system cables, as well as the copper pipes which connect the various brewery tanks.

A steel partition now displays the Freedom logo. Heavy silver-painted structural columns have bolted-on collars of steel coat hooks. The long stainless-steel bar was manufactured in Germany and welded together on site to form one continuous piece. A raised, tilted, back-lit mirror gives an unusually clear view of the space behind you without the normal clutter of bottles and bartenders getting in the way. The combination of cool fluorescent light and shiny stainless steel is peculiarly thirst-inducing. The layout of the wood floor, left over from its days as the shop Space

BOA (Ed Barber and Jay Osgerby) 1998

Freedom Brewing Company

BOA (Ed Barber and Jay Osgerby) 1998

NK, makes little sense with the present-day design but adds another visible layer of site history.

Plain birch plywood has been moulded into a number of different shapes to form curved single benches (which are not uncomfortable after all); simple tables with lipped edges; hollow rolls which serve as bar-height leaning fixtures; and the newly added longer benches which have undeniably comfortable padded seats in steel grey and exaggerated high backs which double as partitions. The feet of the benches were dipped in black paint to avoid unsightly but inevitable scuff marks.

Of course, it all merely forms a backdrop for the huge spotlit copper tanks. Incidentally, it all starts in the hefty brewing tanks (2.5 tonnes when full) which can be seen upstairs at ground level. The ale then travels to the fermentation tanks (behind the glass partition), where it rests for two to four weeks. A full-time brewmaster monitors its progress, which seems to involve a lot of beer ending up on the floor. It travels next to smaller tanks by the bar, from where it is emptied directly into your glass.

ADDRESS 41 Earlham Street, London WC2 (020 7731 7372)
UNDERGROUND Covent Garden
OPEN Monday to Saturday, 12.00–23.00, Sunday 12.00–22.30

BOA (Ed Barber and Jay Osgerby) 1998

Freedom Brewing Company

BOA (Ed Barber and Jay Osgerby) 1998

Saint

At its best this bar is full, pumping and fantastically trashy. Peacocking men and sun-bedded women strut their stuff between the funnel-shaped wooden pillars and glowing purple panels. At its worst early on a weekday evening, without the spacey yet perversely intriguing clientele, the naked space looks as if it had wanted to be so much more, but somehow, somewhere along the way, conceded to its prosaically challenged final state.

The curved booth seating – in slightly off shades of wide-vale corduroy reminiscent of baby-buggy accessories – would have looked great in an expressive pastel sketch; or the naff wall lamps with fussy trailing bits might have looked interesting not in real life. The rusty slug-shaped thing clinging to the entrance-hallway ceiling could have been described at some point as a slithering serpentine structure tempting all to partake in the enticing forbidden pleasures below. The wicker chairs were probably meant to give a contrasting texture to the differently upholstered seats in the dining area but they would really be more at home in a catalogue-furnished suburban lawn. Vaguely traditional-looking dimpled green glazing to the skylit parts of the ceiling adds to the confusion. Is the semi-opaque double-glass screen supposed to look like angel wings? At least this would make some sort of sense. The majestic scale of the entrance stairs down into the bar and the dramatic height of the ceiling before it plunges down to the basement level could have resulted in something architecturally astonishing. Instead, a plain mall-like wood glass and steel balustrading blends into blandness. Bring your own futuristic glamour.

ADDRESS 8 Great Newport Street, London WC2 (020 7240 1551)
UNDERGROUND Leicester Square
OPEN Monday to Thursday, 17.00–1.00; Friday, 17.00–2.00; Saturday, 19.30–2.00

Paul Daly 1996

Saint

west end

Paul Daly 1996

AKA

The owner of The End club next door opened this bar with a definite image of his market – a halfway house for retired clubbers not yet ready to face spending long evenings at home. Kicked upstairs by the kids next door, they don't have very far to go. Its 7 am music and entertainment licence means that even club-lagged schedules are accommodated to make the transition of the youth-challenged as smooth as possible.

The site started out in the nineteenth century as a post office. Underground tunnels for horses were connected to other post offices. Before the present fit-out, ramps leading to the first floor, where the horses slept, still existed. One can see remnants of this history still on the wall. Mysterious areas of red paint, new and old bricks with layers of plaster and small stencilled letters spelling 'KING'S CROSS', 'CAMDEN' and other areas are still easily readable.

A concrete back wall has been treated with pigments, producing a textured golden beige with bluey-grey patches which look a bit like damp. The floor is an ultra-smooth polished dark-blue concrete. Although it has been photographed filled with furniture and there are plans to incorporate leather loungers, on one early evening most of the expanse was left clear except for a sharp row of dark-blue velvet high-backed banquette seating and opposing black plywood Starck chairs. This gave the place a cool barren atmosphere which brought out the beautiful contrast between the grungy walls and the rich finish of the newer parts. This disparity gives the design an edge and keeps it from being just another swanky London bar. The 15-metre-long bar has an angled enamelled zinc front and a top embedded with small fibre-optic lights which quietly change colour through the use of a central kaleidoscope. This is often only noticeable when you look at the changing hues of your Hoegaarden and remember it is the strongest thing you've had all evening.

Douglas Paskin (PKS) and David Connor 1998

AKA

Douglas Paskin (PKS) and David Connor 1998

AKA

The just-visible kitchen and first-floor restaurant occupy a new extension built in an area which was once a courtyard. A mesh balustraded walkway leads to a suspended deck big enough for just one large table. This gives the main bar space even more of an edge as one can feel the overlooking eyes of the dining voyeurs above. The many angles in the space and many triangles in the graphics match the angular letters of the club's name – the logo being formed from the residual spaces of the letters AKA. Wide grooved steel doors lead to the stainless-steel toilets downstairs which have a navy Dalsouple flooring with the minutest of dimples. There is a 4-metre retractable screen which means you might watch the videos you had wanted to watch at home but – with the logic of George Costanza – since you're not at home you can safely claim you are 'doing something'. In addition, just because the music is no longer a pumping 'ince, ince, ince' does not mean the good sound system is wasted. Dionne Warwick sounds delightfully superb on it and fills the space with music not worth shouting over – altogether an extremely civilised way to while away the hours until sunrise.

ADDRESS 18 West Central Street, London WC1 (020 7836 0110)
CLIENTS Layo Paskin, Richard Brindle, Richard West, Douglas Paskin
UNDERGROUND Tottenham Court Road
OPEN Monday, 18.00–1.00, Tuesday to Thursday, 12.00–16.00, 18.00–3.00; Friday, 12.00–3.00; Saturday, 18.00–3.00

Douglas Paskin (PKS) and David Connor 1998

Freud

2.38

A pioneer minimalist bar design, this is a reminder of the almost antediluvian industrial aesthetic of hard-edged concrete which existed long before the insipid-by-comparison stripped pine, muted glass and pebble-strewn shop-sprayed MDF surfaces repeatedly used today in the name of the little 'm' word. The sixteenth-century Venetian woodcut font used for the logo – note the intimidating 'V' instead of the pedestrian 'U' – immediately conjures up images of other 1980s icons, the Mackintosh chair and Cinni fan, which were sold exclusively from the linked shop above.

Originally an Italian cake shop, the space was stripped and the floor lowered, giving the impressive ceiling height which emphasises its cold, austere and hollow crypt-like character. The floor is tiled in a dark green Cumbrian slate – which David Freud obsessively sourced to the quarry which supplied the stone for the chapel floor at St Katherine's College in Oxford. The concrete bar is topped in black Italian slate.

The design has not dated badly. It has lost its edge – literally in the case of the corner of the bar whose concrete has worn away, exposing the embedded steel-mesh reinforcement. Cracks have appeared everywhere and the grey-blue concrete has mellowed to a yellowish tinge. Someone has even caringly added leather pads to the concrete seating, destroying the line but saving our *derrières*. Cinni ceiling fans continue to air the place. They now crank away merely to provide comfort, bereft of the designer object-of-desire status they once had. Refurbishment is imminent: let us pray Freud will not be billing itself as a lounge.

ADDRESS 198 Shaftesbury Avenue, London WC2 (020 7240 9933)
CLIENT David Smith
UNDERGROUND Tottenham Court Road, Covent Garden
OPEN Monday to Saturday, 11.00–23.00; Sunday, 12.00–22.30

Basil Smith 1986

Basil Smith 1986

Jerusalem

The client's brief was for a West End Cantaloupe (see page 4.16). However, the real inspiration behind the design is an old bar in Clignancourt, Paris. The bar had always been owned by a couple who saw no need to refurbish, but just added things or replaced bits which had broken or become obsolete. In this way, the couple held court around their piano and their world was safe from the impact of any drastic changes. Designer Shaun Clarkson wanted to recreate this feeling of a progressive sort of eclecticism in the design of Jerusalem – the look which a place acquires if it has outlived several decades of design trends.

If Jerusalem looks older than its one-and-a-half years then the design has succeeded. The aim was to achieve a faded glamour. If one were to chronologise the parts – the gilt-framed menus look oldest, together with the dark wood cabinet salvaged from the 1930s. This is empty; a mundane cash register sits on it. Next in age is supposed to be the bar itself. This is made of concrete poured directly from the lorry. (This proved tricky: during the first attempt the vibrations from the churning action broke the mould and concrete poured everywhere, including all over the newly laid block resin floor.) The bar is evidently modelled after a 1950s design Clarkson saw in the South Bank Centre. The brick piers supporting a horizontal surface, also of poured concrete, look new and incongruous but this is supposedly the point. The kitchen sits behind red walls with a clean modern horizontal glass slit. This would be the latest addition. The chunky wooden Indian furniture is of no particular era, but it looks exactly as though it comes from medieval times as depicted in computer games. The strange spherical cages of candles look like a bundle of bonus life-energy points or perhaps an even better prize: golden 'run-faster' sandals or 'kill-double-headed-monster-instantly' sabres.

Go on a week night when Jerusalem is relatively empty. The incon-

Jerusalem

Shaun Clarkson 1997

gruous parts look more effective. It is better if it doesn't feel like a particularly popular place – impossible at weekends as it's really pumping. Each detail then takes on the atmosphere of an individual character who has stories to tell. It would be nice to think that London bars weren't so dependent on keeping jam-packed. Imagine a bar that could continue to exist because a few loners liked it …

ADDRESS 33–34 Rathbone Street, London W1 (020 7255 1120)
CLIENT The Breakfast Group Ltd
UNDERGROUND Tottenham Court Road
OPEN Monday to Thursday, 12.00–2.00; Friday, 12.00–3.00; Saturday, 19.00–3.00

Shaun Clarkson 1997

Shaun Clarkson 1997

Office

Although a healthy dose of creativity is easily detected in the design of this bar, it suffers from an overall dinginess and general slackness in the upkeep which hinders appreciation of some of the more curious details. The brief was to provide a Jekyll-and-Hyde venue where suits would feel comfortable in the day – doing their own suity things – but where a wild and crazy younger crowd would groove at night. Of course, there are inherent problems in this arrangement. For instance, scuffed walls and fixtures and a sticky floor might be OK for a clubby atmosphere. In fact, it might even be attractive in a 'if there's beer recklessly spilt all over the floor we must be having a really good time' kind of way. In the cold light of day, the stickiness simply makes one question just how much fun those student days actually were.

An admirable attempt to make the narrow entrance inviting was undertaken by laying a new resin floor and stairs and cutting an opening into the facing wall which allows for a shoulder-height preview of those within. This cut-out theme is continued inside on both the ceiling and wall spaces, which is appropriate in a dark basement bar where differentiating which way is up has little purpose.

Still more cut-outs are to be found in the wood-panelled Formica base cabinet of the bar itself. These have U-shaped frames in dark wood and are illuminated from within by hidden lights.The bar top is a sandwich of laminated Perspex and fluorescent acrylic which sits on an aluminium sheet. This is top-lit by an ultraviolet light, giving the edges an appealing futuristic glow, an effect not unlike that of furniture pieces by designers Proctor and Rihl. A Dalsouple studded flooring has been laid in geometric cut-out patterns in black, orange and yellow (according to the designer this is actually purple, terracotta and ochre). Originally the lozenge-shaped, film-lined back patio doors were meant to create a 'digital wall-

Stephen Donald Architects 1997

west end

Stephen Donald Architects 1997

paper' screen showing computer-generated designs but, sadly, this has never been used.

Furniture is too depressing to mention. Just imagine the kind of stuff that cheap tourist coffee/snack shops near Leicester Square use. The ugliness of the chairs and tables defies you to stay but do return as there is hope. Plans are under way to replace the furniture with specifically designed and adaptable pieces which include cherry- and hardwood-veneered plywood benches with comfy upholstered vinyl pads.

ADDRESS 3–5 Rathbone Place, London W1
(020 7636 1598)
CLIENT Nicholas O'Dwyer
UNDERGROUND Tottenham Court Road
OPEN Monday to Friday, 12.00–3.00, Saturday, 21.30–3.30 (happy hour Monday to Friday, 17.00–19.30)

Stephen Donald Architects 1997

Mash

Often described as futuristic, the design of this micro-brewery bar and restaurant in an ex-Vauxhall garage space is really an image of the future as conceived in the past. The mood is reminiscent of the flowing forms of work by Oscar Niemeyer and fellow Brazilian Roberto Burle Marx from the 1950s, and certain details – for example, the opaque polygon-shaped flush lighting panels on the ceiling – have more to do with the 1950s and 1960s designs of Italian architect Gio Ponti than any current notions of, say, energy-efficient high-tech materials or virtual space.

Mash's façade is set back from its neighbours by 2.5 metres – most probably as a result of public fear or distaste for anything modern. This façade within a façade is successful but the reason for it is somewhat disheartening – restrictive planning regulations that effectively curtail innovation so that something new-looking must draw into itself in an non-confrontational manner.

Past this enclosed set-back with bento box take-away counter to the left and easy-to-swallow coated-tablet-shaped red reception opening on the right, this is an undeniably and brashly modern space with clean comfortable lines and few hard edges. The aesthetic is thorough – at one point even the orange soap had a curvaceous shape – no historical site references have been retained and the space is dominated by smooth curves everywhere one would expect the usual corner detail. This has not resulted, as one might assume, in blobby shapelessness but in rather elegant and fluid stretched forms. For instance, the shelves on the lime-green entrance walls and the telephone kiosks in the pebble-screeded stairwell both look as if they were made of a pliable material which has somehow been pulled out from the walls. Small vents have the reverse effect, as if the material of the walls has been sucked into the gaps. The bar itself is a repeat of the tablet-shaped opening at reception but in a

Andy Martin 1998

Mash

west end

Andy Martin 1998

light-wood colour. The interior of the bar has a highly reflective chrome finish with square (cornerless) openings for bottles and glasses. The row of U-shaped maroon banquettes, organically curved in section, are refreshingly not pushed up against a wall, positioning which highlights their sculptural form. Chairs have simple shapes, as if a thick piece of cut-out foam has been bent in half and set by dipping in a liquid which has then hardened to a rubbery matt green texture. Tables are plain light wood with a single chrome leg which looks like a giant drop of mercury. The back wall is dominated by the large gleaming brewing tanks.

A sunken area on the right has an eye-catching backlit image from a 1970s ad with all the plastic frozen smiles replaced by evil frowns and smirks. This space is furnished with low green banquettes and stools with soft rectangular dimples, and short glass-topped coffee tables (with more mercury-drop legs). The overall effect is that of a lobby/reception of a 1970s ad agency where office parties are attended by characters whose domestic lives revolve around suburban key-parties.

The infamous loos have convex-mirrored urinals and the instant video relays to the women's loos should stop most men from lingering too long over the flattering reflection. As you leave, if you missed the love-machine sayings look back instead to catch inspiring phrases such as 'Jesus loves you but he'll never leave his wife' to propel you into the rest of the night.

ADDRESS 19–21 Great Portland Street, London W1 (020 7637 5555)
CLIENTS Gruppo Ltd (Oliver and Siobhan Peyton)
UNDERGROUND Oxford Circus
OPEN Monday and Tuesday, 11.00–1.00; Wednesday to Saturday, 11.00–2.00

Andy Martin 1998

west end

Andy Martin 1998

R K Stanley

2.52 Within this temple to sausage there is an affable section where the sole sustenance available is of the liquid sort. The eye-catching stainless-steel altar to draught beer has a light source flush with the drip tray so each glass vessel miraculously lights up to highlight the golden liquid within, as if it were infused with a powerful energy which could be captured and harnessed for one's own restorative purposes – and pleasure.

The chrome taps gleam wickedly. The wooden bar surrounded by red padded-leather swivel bar stools stops everyone from rushing to help themselves. Its lipped surface wraps around the altar and carries on deep into the space. As you pivot back and forth expectantly, take the opportunity to notice your beautiful surroundings. The walls are lit by recessed lighting set close enough to cast dark shadows on to the sculptural indentations of the concrete tiles – a repetitive pre-Colombian Mexican pattern via Frank Lloyd Wright. Columns are fluted in contrasting wide and narrow bands which are repeated on the bar front and side walls. Floors are in solid pink terrazzo with dense black, white and beige aggregate and a thin black line around the perimeter of the room. The booths, which could easily be 1950s rock 'n' roll church pews, have a wood frame on angled steel-tube legs and are upholstered in wide-ribbed red leather. The large, black curved-disc lampshades hanging from deep square recesses make the ceiling look vaguely like that of a 1960s auditorium. The staff are dressed in forest ranger/highway patrol-style uniforms giving the place a slight John Waters/David Lynch surreal American campness.

ADDRESS 6 Little Portland Street, London W1 (020 7462 0099)
CLIENT Fred Taylor
UNDERGROUND Oxford Circus
OPEN Monday to Saturday, 12.00–15.00, 18.00–23.00

Quentin Reynolds 1997

R K Stanley

west end

Quentin Reynolds 1997

China White

An intoxicating space made all the more heady by its clandestine location, tucked away deep in the cellars of Café Royal. It is eerily difficult to get your bearings even after you sit down. It feels simultaneously away from it all and in the middle of it all. The enormous size of the highly theatrical main space is intriguingly broken down into many different parts which have your head spinning as you try to decipher them. Exciting and illicit things must surely be happening behind the closed draped seating or below the large tilted silk umbrellas. Low seating melds into banquettes, into platforms, and then into beds, lounges and tables. A mysteriously accessed corridor can be seen snaking around behind these at the back of the space. The relatively brightly lit bar is to one side and for more upright conversations one can walk behind it and sit below the two chimes which hang, waiting for an exotic breeze to blow.

Two shipping containers of materials and furnishings were sourced in Bali and imported by the client. The obvious bits are the deep dark wooden furniture, hand-carved timber doors, stone reliefs, and timber screens. In addition, there is the limestone flooring and teak parquet floor tiles. The thick stone bricks were hand-carved in Bali with the bar's insignia. Light behind the gaps in the bricks invites one to explore for hidden rooms – and there are many, each larger than the next. A *feng shui* expert was consulted but never mind the evil spirits getting lost around these corners, many earthly revellers would too, probably resulting in multiple serendipitous party crashes. The best space is actually down past the entrance before the loos, where a lounge bed – neither queen- nor king-size but more royal-family-and-entourage-plus-assorted-courtesans-size – takes up most of the room. Appropriately, one European princess has been seen cavorting among the ikat pillows.

The loos themselves – equipped with everything from hand lotion to

Munkenbeck & Marshall/interior designer Cara Satmoko 1998

China White

Munkenbeck & Marshall/interior designer Cara Satmoko 1998

Wrigley's – are a row of wooden doors against pale cream smooth stone tiles. This reveals an influence that is more Balinese luxury hotel than Bali proper as the design is straight out of the poolside loos at the Amankila resort. Water to wash … no, bathe your hands flows over an expanse of green pebbles. A rough-hewn stone urinal backsplash was once accidentally combined with high water pressure, dousing an unlucky few.

It is likely that a certain seediness will creep in after a while, but that is something to look forward to as a certain crumpledness will only make the place sexier.

ADDRESS 6 Air Street, London W1 (020 7343 0040)
CLIENT Rory Keegan
UNDERGROUND Piccadilly
OPEN Monday to Saturday, 8.00–3.00; members only at the weekend

Munkenbeck & Marshall/interior designer Cara Satmoko 1998

China White

Munkenbeck & Marshall/interior designer Cara Satmoko 1998

The 'Ten' Room

A lot of hype went with the launch of this place – a fury of PR, an annoyingly slick brochure full of vacant promise and an assortment of magazine articles touting its ab fabness. Sadly it turns out to be just a room – just a painted room. Think of a sad painted clown. The brightness of colour does not conceal the emptiness. Apparently, the brief was 'hugs and kisses' – presumably the space should have felt like an embrace yet the lack of smaller, more intimate areas together with the dull uniformity of the recessed ceiling lights make it feel more like a cold, limp and somewhat insincere handshake.

The only delineation of space comes from a ring of columns that surrounds an inner room. However, the low-back seating throughout and the just-visible backless benches between the columns mean everything is flat and on one level. It is a little like a playschool activity room where shorthanded supervisors need to keep an eye on all the toddlers at the same time. What it needs are some hide-and-seek props and a place for show-offs.

Casualness must have been the intention behind the haphazard arrangement of chairs yet this only implies a casualness in layout. Circulation is awkward and probably would have benefitted from a central catwalk from entrance to bar, which would at least have supplied a little strutting people-watching entertainment. Everyone here seems to be sitting around waiting – for an ex-actress from *EastEnders* perhaps – yet the place has less flair or atmosphere than an economy-class departure lounge.

The deep rich colours – magenta, royal purple and scarlet reds – might appear luxurious when described (or with the right film in your camera) but in reality the matt finishes look tired. Designer Shaun Clarkson had wanted to use the mattness of the paint to distract from the mouldings

Shaun Clarkson 1999

The 'Ten' Room

Shaun Clarkson 1999

and fussy original detailing and to give it a contemporary flatness. The result is unglamorous – as if dyeing an old cheap suit pink is going to make it look modern. If you want to lounge, go home.

ADDRESS 10 Air Street, London W1 (020 7734 9990)
CLIENT City Bars and Restaurants plc
UNDERGROUND Piccadilly Circus
OPEN Monday to Saturday, 18.00–3.00

The 'Ten' Room

Shaun Clarkson 1999

Cheers

A fantastic concept really. A TV show based entirely on the coming and goings of a bar. Bar as metaphor and stage for complex human interaction. Now take this one step further. Feed it back out there – actualise the sitcom, bring this small space which has been appearing in everyone's living room and make it real space. TV show and then the bar. No, this is not a tacky tourist theme bar but a triumphant piece of contemporary pop art. Just look at that fourth wall.

OK, not everyone knows your name and you can wait as long as you like but you won't get a chance to yell 'Norm' as he walks in through the door. But if you are sick of both retro furnishing and futuristic looks, then this it – forget the Dome, this is the *Zeitgeist* of the new millennium right here on Regent Street. Drink in a TV show.

ADDRESS 72 Regent Street, London W1 (020 7494 3322)
UNDERGROUND Piccadilly Circus
OPEN Monday to Wednesday, 12.00–1.00; Thursday to Saturday, 12.00–3.00; Sunday, 12.00–22.30

Pete Project 1998

Cheers

Pete Project 1998

mayfair/st james's

57 Jermyn Street

This bar takes the name of the street which in turn takes its name from Henry Jermyn, Earl of St Albans, who was granted Crown land by King Charles II. He apparently found favour with the king as a result of his relationship with Charles' mother, Henrietta Maria, of whom he is reported to have been a secret husband ... ahhhh, the historical richness of Royal London – it sounds like it's been swinging for some time.

According to Woodward and Jones in *A Guide to the Architecture of London*, when St James's was being laid out, streets and squares were 'designed as settings for fashionable perambulation'. Jermyn Street still conjures up images of gentlemanly things such as cufflinks, shaving and grooming implements, tobacconists and 'bespoke' this and that. Clearly, you arrive at a bar on this street brimming with preconceptions.

With a lack of obvious signage at ground level, this basement bar is easily missable in a way which only adds to its sense of intrigue. The long thin entrance corridor further heightens anticipation so that by the time you arrive at the main space you are convinced there must be something seductively secret happening. The layout is simple with its repetitive rows of U-shaped banquettes which lead to the bar, originally designed for the previous occupant, Tramp. The interior is in a style caught somewhere between the smoky dens of the Prohibition 1930s and a slightly too clean-cut – too tastefully co-ordinated – designery aesthetic. One almost wants to see cigarette burns or wine stains in the beige upholstery or the pristine dark wood surfaces. The ceiling is moodily up-lit to emphasise the curved vault. Additional lighting is provided by charming little lamps with tapered dark wood bases and oblong wicker shades. Placed as a focal point at each table, they cast a conspiratorial yellowy hue on the faces of those seated around it. The deep-red lacquered elliptical tables – glossy enough for a prostrate model in a Helmut Newton shoot – are made by

Quentin Reynolds 1998

57 Jermyn Street

Quentin Reynolds 1998

the people who are responsible for the finish of Steinway pianos. Other seating includes soft cube chairs with simple wooden bar backs.

The walls behind the booths on the right, which are aligned with the end of the tables facing out, are built up to follow the curves of the banquettes. In the centre of each wall space sits a smoky purplish gauzy fabric screen behind which glows a light, giving the illusion of other private spaces. The women's bathroom has an undeniably beautiful large sink in curved solid teak with a slightly Japanese feel to it.

The menus are refreshing – cheap and nasty in bargain-basement office-supply purple plastic – but before one sighs with relief at this relaxation from the hyper-elegance of it all, these too are to be replaced by unbearably luxurious Louis Vuitton covers.

The only real design flaw is in the look of the clientele. One would really wish to see groups of powerful, bald, overweight, and slightly sinister men presiding at each table, with a collection of incredibly young and glamorous molls by their side. In fact the bar attracts a rather neutral, mildly vacant-looking media crowd.

ADDRESS 57 Jermyn Street, London W1 (020 7430 1990)
CLIENTS Henry Besant and Ian Alexander
UNDERGROUND Piccadilly Circus, Green Park
OPEN Monday to Friday 12.00–22.30

57 Jermyn Street

Quentin Reynolds 1998

Che

The Economist group of buildings was the first piece of contemporary architecture to be listed by the Ministry of the Environment. The work of two of the most influential young British architects at the time, Alison and Peter Smithson, dubbed the new Brutalists, was notable in part for the way it successfully fit in with its eighteenth-century neighbours yet still abided with its client's overriding principle that 'there should be no fake antiquarianism in St James's Street'.

Thirty-five years later the brief for the refurbishment of the first two floors of the four-storey bank building into the bar, cigar bar and restaurant Che must have read like a microcosmic version of this – no fake token modernism in the Economist building. With its daunting architectural pedigree and its dedication to the charismatic revolutionary hero Che Guevara, there was much to live up to and the architects have wisely opted to keep it simple and subtle. The barely noticeable references which work well in terms of scale and positioning are to do with the original 1960s banking interior with its timber partitioning and joinery details as well as the relationship between the furniture layout and the existing rhythm of the large windows.

The actual black granite-topped bar is framed by two large, thick, dark-walnut walls which mimic the floor pattern of the original banking hall above. In contrast to the set-back tower of the Economist offices, the Smithsons' smaller building fronts right on to the street and therefore – using a basic module of 3.2 metres – was kept to the same square proportions as its neighbours. In the new interior, the square proportions have been loosely interpreted in the blocks of the colourful light installation behind the bar by Martin Richman. This dominates the space and is easily visible from the street. Pink, red, orange, blue and white light glow from behind smaller opaque panels creating a framing effect for the stacks of

Fletcher Priest 1998

Fletcher Priest 1998

three-dimensional boxes which enclose an impressive selection of liqueurs. Brown leather banquettes have cut-out head rests which allow a compromise between privacy – to avoid Rupert-Sheldrake-style experiments happening from the street – and curiosity, as most people tend to want to look back out.

The cigar lounge downstairs is a cool and subdued space in muted browns and beiges with suede walls and box tables minimally lit by single candles. Built-in dark wood humidors line one wall which has been angled inward to lead the eye to a single, small, framed picture which hangs in the far corner. This portrait of Che is chosen from a seldom-published private collection and is changed regularly to accompany your Cohiba. Most of the art that hangs on the wall refers to well-known pieces of pop art from the 1960s. It would be nice to think that the idealists of the modern movement would be pleased to see the public use of one of its landmarks. Ironically, there has been unofficial approval from the original demanding neighbours as occasional visits from the members of the eighteenth-century club (Boodles) next door have been noted, bringing the story to a tidy full circle.

ADDRESS 23 St James's Street, London SW1 (020 7747 9380)
CLIENT Hani Sarsi
UNDERGROUND Green Park
OPEN Monday to Friday, 11.00–23.00; Saturday, 17.00–23.00

Che

Fletcher Priest 1998

Kemia

This basement bar is a darker, more intense and altogether headier version of the restaurant space upstairs. As one furtively slips past the entrance and down the steep narrow stairs, the beautiful latticework of the ground floor is replaced by sandy-textured plaster walls atmospherically lit by low lights carved out at ankle height. The air is subtly infused with incense and it feels as if one is entering the surreptitious midnight world of the more presentable and public space above. Wide doors painted to look old have chunky iron latches and hinges. Inside, the low undulating ceiling of the vaulted cavernous space makes you instinctively slouch on one of the many sofas. This was once a bomb shelter – a lot of concrete had to be removed as the ceiling was originally a mere two-metres high. The classic colourful Moroccan tinted-glass lamps are concentrated at the actual bar and are partially obscured by the striped silk fabric which hangs from the low ceiling. This makes the bar a natural place for migration, like the temptingly lit tent-stalls of a midnight souk. Unfortunately, drinks can not be bartered for; the presentation of a credit card is preferred.

The decorative stuccoed plasterwork in earthy colours was hand-painted on site but everything else has been sourced from Morocco, Cairo or Istanbul. This includes the large circular brass and wooden trays which sit on the traditional hexagonal tables, the giant brass bowls which serve as sinks in the loos, the metal grillwork encasing the vents and even the soft stool-tables in which are embedded small video screens. Intoxicating music and cocktail versions of traditional mint tea add greatly to the Mahgrebi ambience.

ADDRESS 25 Heddon Street, London W1R (020 7434 4040)
UNDERGROUND Piccadilly Circus
OPEN Monday to Thursday, 18.30–1.00; Friday and Saturday, 18.30–3.00

Sophie Douglas of Fusion 1997

Sophie Douglas of Fusion 1997

ICA bar

Quite a demanding brief was set for the refurbishment of this bar: it had to be buildable in five days and appeal to everyone from Whitehall civil servants to 21-year-olds looking for a hip pre-club venue. On top of this there is probably a core group of fastidious ICA members who have loyally supported the institute over the years and who would be expecting nothing less than a cutting-edge marvel of a creation.

The designers were keen not to alienate anyone so they have come up with an empty slate, or maybe more appropriately an empty, white wipe-clean board of a space. The location and layout of the bar is the same as its predecessor, though it now sits above the New Media Centre. The designers describe the feel of the old place as 'a dated and vain environment with a huge mirror and terrible furniture'. One drawback now is that one feels some pressure to use the space creatively. Just to meet for a few pints doesn't seem good enough. One should perhaps be teleconferencing via one's mobile on an arty surrealist subject or paging someone across the room with an idea for a novel/website/film fest.

Huge white porcelain slabs are supposed to be recognised as the white fireclay slabs of urinals – easier for one half of the population than the other. The Robin Day polyprop chairs have recently gone through a Sunday-supplement revival. But these have been specially commissioned to bypass the colour-injection process, leaving them in their original translucent state, and have clear lacquer-coated steel legs. These are meant to be easy cultural reference pointers to 'conflicting contexts' that any ICA visitor worth their daypass should be able to register.

Walls are panelled in Hexalite which breaks up the backlit picture behind it into a honeycomb pixillated image, making it seem somehow more digital. The bottom panes of the existing windows have been blocked with semi-opaque film which make them look like Muji plastic.

ICA bar

Tables are of standard laminated birch plywood but have been cut – by a computer-controlled routing machine – into pieces which form a section rather than a plan, creating an unusual striped surface from the visible end grain of back-to-back plywood pieces. Lighting has gone a step further from the pragmatic use of exposed galvanised conduits; it forms almost decorative free-standing lamp features which extend horizontally from low beams.

Although the designers' programme of 'collaging new spaces from contemporary experience' might not be readily apparent, they have cleverly put the ball in the punters' court to cope with the encumbering brief.

ADDRESS The Institute of Contemporary Arts, The Mall, London SW1 (020 7930 8619)
CLIENT Philip Owens
UNDERGROUND Charing Cross, Piccadilly Circus
OPEN Monday, 12.00–13.00; Tuesday to Saturday, 12.00–1.00; Sunday, 12.00–22.30 (Sunday brunch 12.00–16.00)

Met Bar

The backlash against the hype surrounding this bar has become so vehement that it should now try angling its selling point as 'so tacky it's cool'. The owners could capitalise on the synthetic atmosphere – akin to an unconvincing movie-set bar – a look which is unconsciously done to perfection here. Their embarrassing efforts included free membership to those deemed to be the 'in' crowd (who unfortunately did not take on board Groucho Marx's infamous put-down). The undeterred few showed up to find: a crackle-glazed Pyrolave bar top in a shiny red to match the equally shiny leather booths and bar stools; a bar front clad in vertical rows of steel tubing; mirrored and Venetian polished-plaster walls; and fumigated oak flooring.

People try hard to have fun here and you can feel the strain of the effort in the air. This would be a good place to wallow in misery. You could really muster up some good wallowing here. A New York cityscape above the booths is meant to ... transport you to the beautiful heady nightlife of the Big Apple circa never, except in the dreams of the young Tony Manero.

ADDRESS Metropolitan Hotel, 19 Old Park Lane, London W1
(020 7447 1000)
CLIENT Ben Reed
UNDERGROUND Hyde Park Corner
OPEN Monday to Sunday, 10.00–17.30

United Designers 1997

Met Bar

United Designers 1997

shoreditch/hoxton

Hoxton Square Bar and Kitchen

The first time I visited this bar, a huge screen covering the entire first-floor façade displayed grazing sheep – an image at once mundane in content yet extravagant in size, and a combination which felt puzzlingly cool yet intriguingly titillating in much the same way as many of the more successful examples of work with the BritArt label. As a result, the bar felt happening and one sat in a naive, expectant posture ready for something experimental to transpire. As it turns out, the screen is not actually part of the bar but belongs to the Lux gallery upstairs. This and the Lux repertory cinema next door are both merely neighbours of the bar in this new building (designed by Maccreanor and Lavington).

The bar entrance is to the side of the floor-to-ceiling glass front. Remember this as you walk out as more than a few have been witnessed trying to push the large panes of glass into becoming doors. There are the obligatory salvaged leather chairs and sofas at ground level when you first walk in and then the space opens downward, doubling in height to accommodate a long *in-situ* concrete bar, a few tables and chairs and then more sofas. A row of paintings is effectively hung at a height which leads the eye – and body, if one could master the art of levitation – straight through without dropping to the once boarded-up ground-level window at the back of the space. This is the focal point of the bar. A fortuitously placed street lamp lights the road outside, creating a stage-like set. The brightness of the car headlights which shine directly into the bar creates a glare, giving occupants the glamorous yet unflattering pallor of a celebrity caught in a paparazzo flash.

But now back to the leather sofas. These are not really all that comfortable, especially when the bar is crowded and one has the misfortune to be squashed beside some arrogant young designer keen to share his views

Andreas Akerlund 1998

Hoxton Square Bar and Kitchen

Andreas Akerlund 1998

on the future of architecture as expressed in the fit-out he's doing for his step-aunt's loo extension ... besides, some knackered, deflated versions are quite difficult to get out of or up from.

ADDRESS The Lux Centre, 2–4 Hoxton Square, London N1 (020 7613 0709)
CLIENT Andreas Akerlund
UNDERGROUND Old Street
OPEN Monday to Saturday, 11.00–24.00; Sunday, 12.00–22.30

Hoxton Square Bar and Kitchen

Andreas Akerlund 1998

Shoreditch Electricity Showrooms

The relaxed personality of this bar has always been its appeal. It possesses the seemingly effortless coolness so desperately sought after by others. The design is not aggressive and it doesn't gloat. A telling sign is the fact that it has changed its trump card – the much-photographed Swiss chocolate-box poster which used to dominate the space. Everyone from Japan to Australia had heard of it so it had to go. It has been replaced – for the time being – by a tree trunk and running-water forest scene.

Significantly, this is one of only a few successful bars that does not aspire to be from another time or place – no one will say it feels like New York, Miami, Prague or 'straight out of the 1970s'. In this respect it appears contented or unaffected, which probably contributes to its popularity – how many bars don't make their clients wish they were somewhere or someone else? Think about it – a state of being normally achievable only through years and years of tearful counselling.

The bar is actually a family-run business designed by University of North London/Architectural Association-trained architect Seng Watson. Since its original incarnation in the 1920s – which explains its Harrod's-style lit dome – as an electricity showroom the building has also housed the mysteriously named 'Urban Response Unit' (as depicted in a gritty monochrome Hackney Council-archive picture). According to Watson, the concept underlying the present design can be found somewhere between these two.

The quirky but subtle ingredients which contribute to the feel of the space include: a stripy entrance mat whose colours are reflected in the wallpaper on a single wall inside; market-found G&E paper lightbox packaging as lampshades; yellow industrial/safety-looking lighting fixtures; and a LED billboard menu depicting bits of trivial information alongside the soup of the day. Furniture is simple – circular tables in

Seng Watson 1998

Shoreditch Electricity Showrooms

Seng Watson 1998

woodgrain Formica with a thick black Formica edge to match the bar and a colour-uncoordinated selection of Eames (four-legged plastic-shell) chairs. The leather sofa-ing of this place has been kept down to a single specimen. A box-shaped shelving unit is built into the wall by the door. There seems to be a reluctance to repeat elements and this encourages the eye to search out the one-offs. Thin rectangular mirrors in the toilets placed at varying heights make one choose to apply lipstick or adjust a collar, but not both.

Genuinely surprised at the almost cult-like following of those desperate to be associated with the Hoxton art scene, this bar seems to have managed simultaneously to generate and to transcend all the hype.

ADDRESS 39a Hoxton Square, London N1 (020 7739 6934)
CLIENT Seng Watson
UNDERGROUND Old Street
OPEN Monday, 18.00–23.00; Tuesday and Wednesday, 11.00–23.00; Thursday, 11.00–24.00; Friday and Saturday, 11.00–2.00; Sunday, 12.00–23.00

Shoreditch Electricity Showrooms

Seng Watson 1998

Home

Together with the now defunct Living Room in Bateman Street, Soho, Home was a pioneer of an aesthetic based on the look and feel of domestic space. Worn sofas and three-piece suites were arranged in cosy groups on a scale similar to that of a typical front room. This was meant to induce feelings of comfort and informality akin to the relaxed atmosphere found at the home of a friend.

Unfortunately, however, the intimate feel has changed recently. The entrance is still the same with its green carpet and glossy magnolia paint. The striped logo of a house outline is still there. But when you go down the stairs, the first room which used to be sparingly furnished with just a few club flyers is now packed with old sofas. Enter the main space and there before you, as far as the eye can see is ... sofa. A close-packed sofa landscape. The highly photogenic set-up of a wide circular cut-out in line with a similarly-sized mirror still intrigues but it is difficult to play with this without tripping over the sofas. The old corner home bar piece which used to be upstairs now sits ineffectually across from the real bar highlighting the ordinariness of its glass-block front.

The use of second-hand leather sofas and the ominous feeling of imminent death-by-protruding-rusty-spring has been tolerable here simply because this bar has been a trailblazer, but if they're not careful the crowding, together with the arrogant and blundering staff, will leave Home's owners dealing with empty-nest syndrome.

ADDRESS 100–106 Leonard Street, London EC2 (020 7684 8618)
CLIENTS Des Byrne and Neil Gregory
UNDERGROUND Liverpool Street, Old Street
OPEN Monday to Friday, 12.00–24.00; Saturday and Sunday, 18.00–24.00;

Home

Des Byrne and Neil Gregory 1997

Great Eastern Dining Room

The rabidly territorial denizens of Hoxton apprehensively watched as this place was fitted out. Was this to be another bar bringing in the shiploads from out west and worst of all from the City who drink our beer and steal our women? Probably inspired by the maxim 'know your enemy', they cautiously filed in, had a good sniff around the sleek premises and then threw themselves against the aluminium bar while victoriously announcing, 'it's ours'.

Although obviously named for the road its on, there is something egalitarian about the name, as if it referred to some common act of toil or bravery like the 'Great Leap Forward', or a source of national pride as in 'Great Barrier Reef'. It has in fact turned out to be the greatest good for the greatest number as a healthy mix of people is usually to be seen happily drinking away within the large and airy space which seems especially conducive to intermingling. By the end of the evening, the stylish but utilitarian-looking dark wooden chairs are usually bunched in a Speakers' Corner crowd pattern around the friendliest groupings which preside from the brown leather banquettes.

The walls are cream with boxed-in areas of dark stained-oak panelling. The space is lit by vintage (early 1970s) chrome Castiglione chandeliers and natural daylight from the large windows which have been uniformly fitted with fluted glass panels. These have the magical effect of turning dreary Great Eastern Street with its rumbling passing traffic into a striped panoramic blur of painterly patterns and lovely abstracted urban forms.

A bit of levity is added by the large black line pictures of characterful waiters which were painted by Australian graphic designer Richard Allen on to the *tricolore* walls in shades which designer Chris Connell refers to as 'knocked out', as in bruised. Peculiar shelves of canned tomatoes

Chris Connell 1998

Great Eastern Dining Room

shoreditch/hoxton

Chris Connell 1998

and red peppers look like an installation paying homage to Andy Warhol's tomato soup can but serve merely as a reminder of the grub available within. The downstairs has recently been turned into a multimedia art/ presentation space, a use which must surely have the Hoxton stamp of approval.

ADDRESS 54–56 Great Eastern Street, London EC2 (020 7613 45455)
CLIENT Will Ricker
UNDERGROUND Old Street
OPEN Monday to Friday, 12.00–24.00; Saturday, 18.00–24.00

Chris Connell 1998

Great Eastern Dining Room

Chris Connell 1998

Cantaloupe

People wearing suits of combat gear, designer trainers and those annoying cross-shoulder contraptions smugly look over at people wearing suits of pin-stripe. Unfortunately the suits do not mix well and the rising tension between the opposing factions means that the suits are too keyed up to realise that they're just two sides of the same mobile phone. Let them fight it out as you sit back and enjoy the high-ceilinged and otherwise easy-going atelier feel of this bar interior.

This is almost a wood-themed bar – not as in different species of woods, but as in format and finish as a mix of chunky rough-stained, old yellowing-varnished and modern new-ply wooden furniture vies for attention. Floors are lacquered chipboard and the bar is composed of a polished dark wood top with a rough stained woodplank front. Behind the bar, wooden shelves are stacked high on a structure of scaffolding and so too are the benches by the windows. Non-wood features include the kitchen service hatch with a sliding shutter which looks semi-industrial in zinc, and the exposed steel-and-zinc ducts against a dark green ceiling. A middle room of leather sofas, potted plants and bubblegum machines leads to the later addition of an inner bar and dining room. Spill out on to the pavement if you have to, but avoid this back area as the design is disturbingly incompatible and could even be mistaken for a Pitcher and All Bar Slugs. Sssssssss!

ADDRESS 35–42 Charlotte Road, London EC2 (020 7613 4411)
CLIENT Richard Big
UNDERGROUND Old Street, Liverpool Street
OPEN Monday to Sunday, 11.00–24.00

Cantaloupe

Richard Big 1997

Dragon Bar

This building was constructed in the 1860s to house a printing workshop but when Justin Piggott found it a couple of years ago it was being used as storage for a local school. He chose the site for its East End Dickensian character but also liked its size and the fact that its three floors would offer a more intimate scale at each level than the single vast open spaces of other sites he had visited. Discoveries such as the mismatched panes of obscured and textured glass – the whole place had been boarded up – and the working fireplaces led to a decision to keep the original character of the building with only minimal interference from new design elements. The idea was to look old but not decrepitly so; various parts could be gradually added, changed and developed from the bare canvas of the original features.

The bar has an *in-situ* concrete base with white plastic-coated wood panels and a sealed concrete top. Hidden lighting is cast downwards at the foot of the base. The rows of bottles on three simple concrete-block shelves are lit by small porthole lights. Trays of low-voltage lamps are encased in a sculptural-looking wing-shaped steel light which hangs from the ceiling on steel wires. The spindly form of the piece is jewellery-like, which is unsurprising as Piggott has previously designed stands for contemporary jeweller Janet Fitch. The large twisted antlers hanging by the door are not – as often claimed by those looking for unusual mannequin body parts – by Jake and Dinos Chapman, who are instead responsible for the skull panels downstairs. It was simply a found piece from Brick Lane proving that the old adage, 'hang it on the wall and call it art', really works! The bony outgrowths are also not part of some mascot or namesake for the bar – the name of which was chosen purely for its Georgian-pub connotations.

The slate step entrance with the discreetly embedded 'Dragon' name

Justin Piggott 1998

Dragon Bar

Justin Piggott 1998

is often accompanied by an intimidating hand-written 'no office clothes' sign. This is apparently not meant to offend but to keep the place from becoming a strictly after-work City bar – the original intention being for a more relaxed drinking venue which local residents would find equally comfortable at different times of the day.

ADDRESS 5 Leonard Street, London EC2 (020 7490 7110)
CLIENT Justin Piggott
UNDERGROUND Old Street
OPEN Monday to Sunday, 11.00–23.00

Justin Piggott 1998

Mother 333

This head-on collision of anarchic elements is meant to be the antithesis of the other bars in the area which, according to the owners of Mother 333, aspire to minimalist loft aesthetics with their rows of 'identical Charles Eames chairs'. The quintessential rows of second-hand leather sofas do look identical after a while but are they Eames?

The entrance walls are plastered with large, bright, thirst-generating prints of juicy apples and oranges. Upstairs the two rooms share a black padded and buttoned leather bar with bar staff moving back and forth along its length and disappearing behind the dividing wall. The first room has large paisley-patterned red and gold wallpaper with one corner covered by a giant denim jeans bum pocket displaying a red 'MOTHER' label where normally one would check for the capital E. The floor is a large black and white checkerboard pattern and the furniture is well ... a mixture – wooden tree-trunk chairs, low Moroccan tables, red and blue leather wavy boxed benches and shockingly ordinary, new-looking leather-upholstered wooden chairs and sofas. The second room has 'Coyote and Roadrunner' landscape posters (Devil's Peak, Utah) pasted haphazardly and covering most walls except for the one behind the bar which is covered with goldleaf and painted with strange mantra symbols. The floor has been painted a patchy dark red and once again the furniture is a mix. Both spaces have odd bits of side furniture including a large steel safe, but these are useful as temporary leaning surfaces and as places to rest your drink. Note the above-bar lighting which is a row of orb-shaped lamps to which have been stuck numerous little bottles of Tanqueray.

The house cocktail is the Dirty Mother, a dirty Martini made with Tanqueray export-strength gin. Look up 'mother' in the dictionary and you'll find a lesser-known second definition which is 'a stringy slime

Vicky Pengilly, Pablo Flack and Ashley Collett 1999

Mother 333

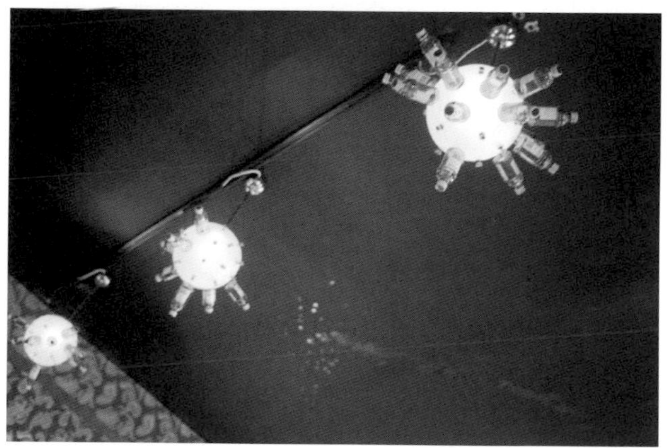

Vicky Pengilly, Pablo Flack and Ashley Collett 1999

containing various bacteria that forms on the surface of liquids undergoing acetous fermentation'. Hmmmm … contemplate this as you decide on your next drink while surveying the elite of local Hoxton – which is the bar's intended clientele – in this motley mother of a space.

ADDRESS 333 Old Street, London EC1 (020 7739 5949)
CLIENTS Vicky Pengilly, Pablo Flack and Ashley Collett
UNDERGROUND Old Street
OPEN Monday to Wednesday, 18.00–1.00; Thursday, 18.00–2.00; Friday, Saturday, Sunday, 18.00–24.00

Mother 333

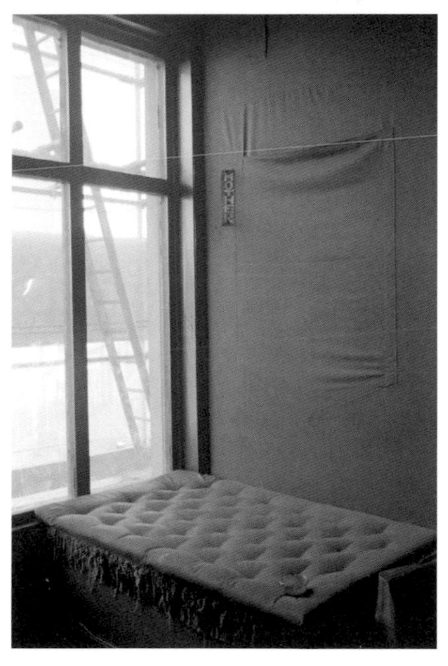

Vicky Pengilly, Pablo Flack and Ashley Collett 1999

clerkenwell

L.e.d.

At first this bar appears to be just another piece of retro design – an unfair assessment but not an unforgivable one as there has been an avalanche of flea-ridden sofas hitting London bars recently. The reason L.e.d. does have the look of the flared decade is probably a little design feature – the cut-off rounded corner. Like that other retro feature, the ubiquitous 1950s amoeba shape, the rectangle without sharp corners – think of a Chiclet – signals to many groovesters that here is a specimen of stylishness.

There is, however, no vintage leather here, no beads, not even cocktail-years bar snacks. The lack of sharp corners is purely to do with the Light-Emitting-Diode theme which, granted, has enjoyed a certain popularity before the present time. The reference is apparently to Clerkenwell's watchmaking history. Although the digital timepiece might seem like an unusual theme for a bar, it actually works. One can imagine the monster that could have been created in the hands of someone with the same theme but less restraint: LED menus, LED signs to the loos, scrolling LED thoughts for the day behind the bar, LED-stamped bar-staff foreheads, LED font everywhere. No, here LED is only used in the clever graphic patterns of the wallpaper. Graphic designer Paul White uses thin red-and-white outlines of LED shapes overlaid at varying scales on to a cardboard-brown background. Fake shadows are printed on the paper, resulting in many waving hands of those curious to find the light source! A bit gimmicky perhaps, but a lack of smugness means it's only playful fun.

The rest of the cut-out corners can be found on the tabletops, door handles, safety-glass windows in the doors, and the little rubber bumps in the beige-green linoleum flooring. The white enamelled-steel bar is simple and clean-looking and is subtly without sharp corners.

The downstairs is a dark, reclining version of the upstairs, only with

Paul White in collaboration with Simon Eckel 1999

L.e.d.

clerkenwell

Paul White in collaboration with Simon Eckel 1999

L.e.d.

PlayStation and two 32-inch flat-screen televisions used for sports events and multimedia presentations. Details are mainly red. Furniture is made of red enamelled-steel sheets bolted together, framing soft black cushy insides. Remarkably, the design concept is not perceived as a repetitive one-liner but rather reads as a subtle feature giving the various details a good sense of unity. The atmosphere – 'analogue sounds in a digital lounge' – is set by guest DJs on Friday and Saturday nights and, if you still need proof of what decade you're in, everything on the menu is organic.

ADDRESS 171 Farringdon Road, London EC1 (020 7278 4400)
CLIENT Riki-Tik
UNDERGROUND Farringdon
OPEN Monday to Friday, 8.00–24.00; Saturday, 10.00–24.00 (happy hours Monday, 16.00–24.00; Tuesday to Saturday, 16.00–20.00)

Paul White in collaboration with Simon Eckel 1999

Paul White in collaboration with Simon Eckel 1999

Café Kick

You can imagine the owner of this place saying, 'I want to open a bar where people come to play my favourite game in the world, table football, and I want it to look like a charming little French bar I know in which I had one of my best games ever ... blah blah blah.' He would talk about the project for years and years and could be relied upon to never really do it, sparing everyone the heartbreaking stories of sinking his last few pennies into a project he was sure other people would like too only ... Well, you'd be wrong.

In fact, the result has been quite successful. The site is an ex-launderette and it turns out that Café Kick isn't the product of anybody's lifelong ambition (though someone's grandfather used to own Fulham Football Club). The row of table-football games (manufactured by René Pierre and imported from Paris) form not only the main focal point in terms of activity but also the main decorative theme. One of the games actually hangs out of reach on the wall for effect, but the other three are quite often seen in use. The functionality of the theme here is very welcome given the trend in bars for the show-only concept. Imagine a Pharmacy where clients could really use the pharmaceuticals.

Furniture includes salvaged wooden football seats on whose backs are painted numbers, black-edged Formica-topped wooden tables, and doors with fluted glass panels (hopefully, rumours that the owners wish to replace these with stained-glass are not true) which divide the area by the bar. Walls are painted cream with red stripes which seems to be a particularly 1950s colour combination, though any conscious effort to achieve a retro look is denied. Manager Gareth Kerr admits that he was after a 'rustic' feel. This sounds worse but luckily he does not mean the 'country-kitchen' look rampant in British suburbia. Other things acquired on excursions to Paris are the World Cup paraphernalia pinned on the walls

Gareth Kerr et al 1997

Café Kick

clerkenwell

Gareth Kerr et al 1997

which unarguably date from the 1950s and 1960s. A colourfully painted wooden floor depicts team flags. Its scratched and scuffed surface gives it the appeal of a much-loved and worn-out wooden toy. In fact the atmosphere feels slightly like that of an old fairytale toyshop – one in which Pinocchio might have lived and where you would expect to see old Giuseppe come out and retract the awning or tinker with the vintage-looking Café Kick clock which protrudes above the entrance. Fortunately, the new JVC television perched in a corner by the bar stops it from looking completely like a set or museum.

The over-riding impression is undoubtedly one of comfort. This probably stems from a certain insouciant devil-may-care impression one gets from such minor details as the uncoordinated power socket and extension cords dangling from one corner and the red silk flower nonchalantly propped up by a bunch of real leaves of unknown origin stuck in an old bottle. It is hard to imagine neon light helping to provide a relaxed atmosphere but here it does, providing the unpretentious feel of a small-town all-night joint with no particular aspirations other than to provide a drink.

ADDRESS 43 Exmouth Market, London EC1 (020 7837 8077)
UNDERGROUND Farringdon, Angel
OPEN Monday to Saturday, 12.00–23.00

Café Kick

clerkenwell

Gareth Kerr et al 1997

Match

5.10

There is no doubt about what exactly the main draw is here. The focus of the below-ground central space (you enter at mezzanine-level which leaves the sunken bar with a dramatically high back wall of obscured glass windows) is the blue back-lit rows of bottles and bottles of enticing cocktail ingredients. Details of the actual fit-out do not attempt to compete and eye-level railings together with the change in level ensure that even the act of people-watching will not distract.

Zinc-panelled walls and original cast-iron columns are painted a deep industrial grey. Dark wood flooring, smooth dark wood tables and chairs and dark brown leather sofas all defer to the spectacle of the bar area. They simply provide a comfortable backdrop and prop for your elbow as you balance another martini in your hand. The backing of the leather-upholstered bench seating even stops midway so as to not obstruct the view from the windowed areas. The playful design of the lighting fixtures is the only other obvious point of interest. Lights are hung from camping-lantern-like handles with telescopic aluminium parts which resemble prawn tails (hopefully no pun intended here). Lights over the tables look like crumpled rolls of mesh. Perhaps the designer was allowed a little inventiveness here: after all, lighting only serves further to highlight the colourful drinks of the mixing Meisters.

ADDRESS 45–47 Clerkenwell Road, London EC1 (020 7250 4002)
CLIENT Jonathan Downey
UNDERGROUND Farringdon
OPEN Monday to Friday, 11.00–24.00; Saturday, 18.00–24.00

Harrison Ince 1997

Harrison Ince 1997

Dust

Ray Brown and Mark Thompson set their own brief here as they juggled the roles of frustrated designer, critical owner, frugal developer and even jolly caterer when dealing with the breweries. Despite local conservation-area restraints which meant the original idea for the entrance layout had to be abandoned, the bar attracts the eyes of passers-by with an ever-changing art display which sits (or hangs) in the deep room-like space by the window. So far this has included a white-painted drum kit and a revolving wireframe human figure which casts engaging moving patterns on to a screen. The bar's concepts of time and water are meant to reflect Clerkenwell's history as a centre for watchmaking – Dust is located in a derelict Victorian watch factory – as well as an area of water supply.

The entrance has a grey, blue and black mosaic floor depicting the Dust logo. The angled wall has rectangular cut-outs which house lighting to the seating area immediately in front of the window. From the far end of the space these look like the openings in a retail display wall at a designer shop – specially constructed and fitted for a single shoe or thigh-high boot.

The opposite wall has original tongue-and-groove boarding and is lined with a long continuous banquette of bent plywood. The bar front is panelled with the same blond wood. An 8-metre-long, 100mm acid-etched deep concrete slab covered in a thick layer of resin makes a unique bar top.

The dining area at the back is a dramatic, double-height space covered by a transparent corrugated-plastic roof. The immense stretch of wall is covered in squares of copper leaf, some of which are just beginning to turn a nice green. Unglazed windows mean the first-floor kitchen can easily be seen, and smelled. With your eyes sky-bound,

Dust

Ray Brown and Mark Thompson 1998

remember to tread carefully as the original uneven floorboards have been retained.

The loos downstairs are astonishingly spacious and even have their own waiting/seating area with a silver-leaf curved wall and mesh-imprinted concrete tiles.

ADDRESS 27 Clerkenwell Road, London EC1 (020 7490 5120)
CLIENTS Ray Brown and Mark Thompson
UNDERGROUND Farringdon
OPEN Sunday to Thursday, 11.30–23.00; Friday and Saturday, 11.30–2.00

Dust

clerkenwell

Ray Brown and Mark Thompson 1998

Cicada

This place seems to have mellowed out pleasantly since the trend-fixated hoi polloi have moved east in search of the fumes of fresh paint. The darkness of this bar is warmly enveloping and the seating soft but not squishy. It brings back memories of a time when new bars did not all want to look 1970s, 'lounge' was not an obligatory feature and irony was just a word wrongly used in an Alanis Morisette song. The year was 1997.

Today, you can still visit this bar and although there are subtle changes in the decor, it has remained more or less the same since its opening. The Pacific Rim was all the rage then and you can still see vestiges of this in the bamboo-fronted bar to the kitchen and 'opium-den' theme of the silk-pillowed, wood-screened space downstairs with its painted sake-barrel wall and gold dragon-fronted bar.

Upstairs, the wooden bar stools look influenced by rural Japanese forms and the beautiful translucent beige Perspex lampshades have a shape suggestive of the gentle curves of a sampan fisherman's straw hat. Wooden booth seats have fluted glass inserts and the black terrazzo floor has fist-sized muddy grey aggregates which look vaguely colonial 1950s. The features are a sort of mish-mash medley but on a cold winter evening the incandescent light of the sculptural fireplace – which looks decidely un-Rim like and more like a Moroccan clay stove – together with the yellowy hues and long shadows of the other light sources, generate a mood that is definitely sultry.

ADDRESS 132–136 St John Street, London EC1 (020 7608 1550)
CLIENT Will Ricker
UNDERGROUND Farringdon
OPEN Monday to Friday, 12.00–23.00; Saturday, 18.00–23.00

Richard Gordon 1997

Cicada

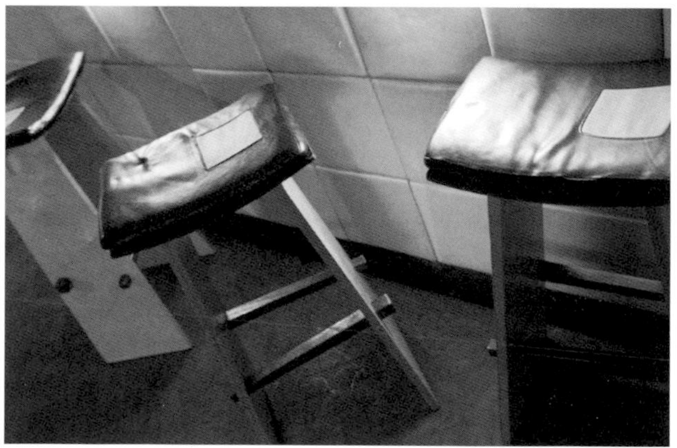

clerkenwell

Richard Gordon 1997

St John

When the owners first visited this site they were confronted by a curious mixture of rubble, pork fat, smoke, and psychedelic wall paintings. Its original incarnation as a bacon smokehouse accounted for the Joseph-Beuys aspect and its later appropriation for all-night raves explains the other artwork. Now the space is airy, clean and white with the comfortable smell of baking bread which brings to notice just how apt a combination beer and bread is. The corridor entrance looks as if it served as a courtyard at one point but is now covered in glass which floods the space with enough natural daylight to spill into the raised dining area. There is still a latticework of smoking racks above the bar which is a simple box in roofing zinc. The concrete floor has an occasional glint as the plan to create a poor man's terrazzo by grinding down a sprinkling of aggregate was scuppered by the too-fast hardening of the concrete. A uniform hanging of factory/warehouse lights spreads between the two spaces.

This bar has a strange architectural significance as its clients are an invariable mixture of architects and architects – throw an Eccles cake behind you and you're sure to hit one. The chef and co-owner is also a trained architect which perhaps accounts for the happy seamless integration of drink, food and design.

ADDRESS 26 St John Street, London EC1 (020 7251 4080)
CLIENTS Trevor Gulliver, Jon Spiteri and Fergus Henderson
UNDERGROUND Farringdon
OPEN Monday to Friday, 12.00–23.00; Saturday, 18.00–23.00

Fergus Henderson 1995

St John

Fergus Henderson 1995

Clerkenwell House

A classic not in its own right. A classic Home-wannabe. Almost infuriating in its lack of effort. After all it takes more than just the ubiquitous leather sofa to make this place a ... Apparently a duo called McCullough & Dye are to blame. They have been pushing the things from their Clerkenwell Road showroom with no quantity control whatsoever so these second-hand sofas are spreading west at ungovernable speed. It's not all their fault though, as they're not responsible for the design of the places they sell to. Still, to foist them on to unsuspecting bar owners who have bought into the promise of comfort and coolness is just not right.

The design has simply come about by letting various external influences guide its course. This lack of direction – abetted by a tiny £40,000 budget – did not result in a funky, wild mutant but instead a plain, unworked-out-looking space which relies heavily on location. It looks semi-inviting from the outside – large panes of dramatically lit glass often do – but once you're inside its plain – but not minimally so – white walls and all-too-even lighting feel like a cheap estate-agent's office or, worse, some quickly set-up emergency room whose only contact with the public is by phone. They were probably also sold the 'loft' word even though the space has none of the industrial-looking details which characterise the loft aesthetic. Come to think of it, it looks as if they have been sold the 'lounge' word too. This is exactly what has happened. They were given the 'buy a sofa, get loft-and-lounge atmosphere for free' hard sell.

ADDRESS 23–27 Hatton Wall, London EC1 (020 7404 1113)
CLIENT Delicious Bar Holdings
UNDERGROUND Farringdon
OPEN Monday to Friday, 12.00–23.00; Saturday, 17.00–23.00; Sunday, 13.00–17.00

Delicious Bar Holdings 1999

Clerkenwell House

Delicious Bar Holdings 1999

the city

Black Friar

This Arts-and-Crafts pub is a bit of an anomaly: disciples of the movement did not usually count alcoholic drink as an object worthy of their attention. Although its site is awkwardly squeezed out from leftover space between the junction of road, bridge, underpass and above-ground railway, the chubby iron-shaped building is home to one of the most flamboyant and quirkily designed drinking venues in London.

The friar theme comes from the Dominican priory which once existed just north of the pub and the men in robes are to be found everywhere. Copper plates have been worked into numerous different scenes in the main room and into even stranger postures and stances in the later addition of an inner Grotto room which was created from the excavated space of a railway vault. Heavily variegated yellow marble pieces form arches, nooks and crannies. The high vaulted ceiling is striped with dark-wood beams and a caramel-coloured glaze which makes it look like a layered dessert. Elsewhere, the ceiling is covered in circular and star-shaped designs made of glistening gold mosaic tiles. A sunrise and friar scene is depicted in stained glass which, together with the smaller panes of uneven rippling glass, gives the pub a chapel-like feel. Mottoes in imposingly large lettering proclaim that 'Haste is slow', 'Finery is foolery' and 'Industry is all', yet most people here are simply drinking to the end of another working day.

ADDRESS 174 Queen Victoria Street, London EC4 (020 7236 5650)
CLIENT Alfred Pettitt
UNDERGROUND Blackfriars
OPEN Monday to Friday, 11.30–23.00; Saturday, 12.00–16.30

H Fuller Clark 1875; refurbishment + extension 1904

Black Friar

H Fuller Clark 1875; refurbishment + extension 1904

Can

Yes, it sounds gimmicky but inoffensively so and it's surprisingly good if you're in the area – which unfortunately is the problem as usually you're not. Once you are here, the large glass façade gives you a clear view of the empty streets surrounding Smithfield market, a welcome change from drinking in better-known, high-frequency-of-others-doing-the-same zones. Borrowing the serene feeling of space from outside, it is with ease that one concentrates on the job at hand – trying the beers of the world.

A large refrigerated vending machine sits behind the bar with the moving racks of colourful cans performing a double act – decorous backdrop *and* providers of refreshing ale. An electronic beerboard presents the latest news on the actual selection. There is a remarkable sense of restraint in the steel blue of the walls as it would have been tempting to paint everything a can-like silver. Downstairs, more vending machines dispense beer-flavoured condoms and disposable cameras. Lockers replace messy coat-check rooms and for once the use of aluminium/chrome loos makes a bit of sense. Windows in the loos look out over stacks of cans – unforgivably arranged to spell 'CAN'. By the entrance, long, tubular can suckers – to which you bring your empties to be crushed – poke out from what used to be the blood pits of the sausage butchers who originally occupied the building. Can crushing is really quite fun and afterwards you can smugly sidle up to the bar again as if you've done your bit for the environment.

ADDRESS 50–52 Long Lane, London EC1 (020 7796 0069)
CLIENTS Steve Switzman and David Strang
UNDERGROUND Barbican, Farringdon
OPEN Monday to Saturday, 17.00–24.00 (but check for private parties on Saturdays)

Jump (Shaun Fernandes and Rene Shavanne) 1998

Jump (Shaun Fernandes and Rene Shavanne) 1998

Le Coq d'Argent

Significant if only for its huge roof-top terrace overlooking the City. This bar (and restaurant) occupies the top floor of the hugely controversial (and hugely pink) James Stirling building which was built instead of what would have been London's only Mies. A bright orange and blue elevator whizzes you up from either ground or Tube level, through the lower floors and 'express' zones, to deliver you into the bright and breezy outdoor space. The actual dark walnut-panelled bar is inside among the usual stainless steel, glass and more dark wood-panelled surfaces. The terrace furniture comprises the same unremarkable wicker and chrome chairs that furnished Conran's own self-promoting exhibit at 1999's Chelsea Flower Show which was billed as a fictitious 'roof-top garden somewhere in the city'. Large cream and wood parasols mean you can sip your G&Ts even if a light rain is falling. Marble tiles and planters glisten but the welcome bits of greenery are the real focus. A large geometric copper roof with a wood-slatted interior and the bright colours of the lightwell façade below try to distract but don't be put off as – in estate-agent speak – location is everything.

ADDRESS No. 1 Poultry, London EC2 (020 7395 5000)
CLIENT Sir Terence Conran
UNDERGROUND Bank
OPEN Monday to Friday, 11.30–23.00; Saturday, 18.30–23.00 (but check for occasional private parties) Sunday, 12.00–15.30

CD Partnership 1998

Le Coq d'Argent

CD Partnership 1998

1 Lombard Street

Another bar sited in what used to be a bank – it sounds like a yawn, but this must surely be the mother of all ex-bank sites. The neo-classical grade-II listed building is home of the Scottish Providence Institution and this bar/brasserie is housed in what used to be its grand banking hall. Ironically, because of its location smack in the middle of the City, there are probably more bankers occupying the space at any given time now than during its previous incarnation.

Although one would expect such a large void to feel draughty, cold or austere, it is in fact a surprisingly warm and comfortable drinking venue, albeit majestically so. The space is dominated by a magnificent giant dome whose three tiers of windows let in so much daylight it is sure to lift, if only temporarily, the gloomiest working day of anyone sitting below it. The dome's shape is echoed by the perfectly circular bar of creamy marble atop a wooden base and a surprisingly futuristic-looking thick-lit column of deal-closing, deal-cementing or just deal-lubricating liquor. Curved mushroom-coloured banquette seats to the side have gold-leaf walls and baby domes of their own.

In the basement there are private rooms with hushed closed doors. The minimally swish loos have a single white orchid at the sinks and floor-to-ceiling mirrors into which one can recite empowering little mantras before going back to the boardroom.

ADDRESS 1 Lombard Street, London EC3 (020 7929 6611)
CLIENT Soren Jessen
UNDERGROUND Bank
OPEN Monday to Friday, 11.00–23.00

Orefeld Associates 1998

1 Lombard Street

Orefeld Associates 1998

notting hill

Pharmacy

For all the hype, this bar does not amount to much more than a simplistic one-liner. Which is OK ... if it's good enough to be called Art then presumably it's good enough to drink in. It does seem to be taken more seriously than other themed establishments though, when its concept is really more or less on the same level of banality as, say, Fashion Café. Inspired by his 'Pharmacy' artwork (circa 1992, seven long years ago), Damien Hirst was responsible for the concept, the production of the artwork and the redesign of the space both internally and externally.

Interior-design gags include classic chemist-yellow, pull-down blinds, walls lined with standard white medicine cabinets, pill-shaped bar stools, glass-fronted urinals stuffed with scissors, tampons, bandages and cotton wool, lightboxes depicting a scattering of pills and various green medical symbols on walls, doors, menus and on the back of chairs. There is a confusion of conflicting light sources with blue ER tube lighting, red lights by a curved red wall, long egg-shaped pendant lights and both regular recessed lighting fixtures and office grid lighting. Hits from more recent times are brought in to decorate the stairwell where there is an array of Damien dots printed on to the windows. Oddly, the gag stops at the reception desk where huge lightbox panels display popular, pretty, nature pictures such as images of clouds, cracked ice and rippling water. Telling quotes include, 'as an artist you have to sell art in order to sustain a kind of lifestyle' and, 'We have a bar which is rocking, which is like, you know ... people vomiting and dropping glasses and dancing and chaos'.

ADDRESS 150 Notting Hill Gate, London W11 (020 7221 2442)
UNDERGROUND Notting Hill Gate
OPEN Monday to Thursday, 12.00–15.00, 18.00–1.00; Friday and Saturday, 12.00–15.00, 18.00–2.00; Sunday, 11.15–15.00, 18.00–22.30

Mike Rundell/Damien Hirst 1998

Pharmacy

Mike Rundell/Damien Hirst 1998

Ion

As part of a North Kensington Amenity Trust regeneration programme (rent here goes towards further regeneration projects in the area), this bar – which alternatively could have been a job centre, shop or office – surprisingly benefits from the Westway whizzing above and the unglamourised streetscape opposite. The surroundings give the space a gritty urban feel, an almost instant ready-made atmosphere and character. It stops the pale, smooth surfaces of the interior from looking too prim, too Mr Clean-jeans. As it is, the space has a light, spacious feel but with the borrowed kick necessary to make it worthy of late-night revelry.

The entrance is through a small, patinated, copper-clad cubicle, polka-dotted with stainless-steel portholes and topped with a shiny copper roof. The main floor is split-level with a first-floor dining mezzanine generously set back to allow the openness of the double-height to dominate. Large windows have frames and deep protruding sills in pale wood which extend externally in copper. More metallic accents can be found in the silver- and gold-leaf walls, stainless-steel bar details, and brass foot- and handrails. The zig-zagging bar – echoing the mezzanine above – is fronted with panels of caramel-coloured leather alternating with green glass and stainless-steel lightboxes and topped by nougat-white terrazzo with coloured-glass aggregate. Unfortunately, the behind-the-bar space is in a bit of a disarray and looks unnecessarily cluttered. Red leather bench/bed furniture (designed by (Jasper Morrison for Cappellini) is vaguely airport-terminal-like (terminally airport?), but comfortable.

A single-storey lift looks disarmingly and expensively high-tech and could have been made a feature but is instead hidden – almost shamefully – behind the cream wall by the folded-steel-plate and oak staircase. A terrace deck on the first floor looks modern (strikingly urban without the

Sproson Barrable 1998

Sproson Barrable 1998

usual forced-looking vegetation) and inviting with simple slatted wood bench seating and patterned aluminium tabletops. There are no guarantees of negative-ion dispensing hugs (as implied by the name?) but who knows what a drink or two might lead to?

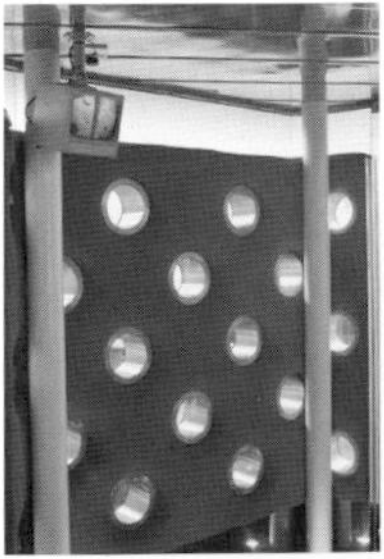

ADDRESS 161–165 Ladbroke Grove, London W10 (0181–960 1702)
CLIENT North Kensington Amenity Trust (tenant, Mean Fiddler)
UNDERGROUND Ladbroke Grove
OPEN Monday to Friday, 17.00–24.00; Saturday and Sunday, 12.00–24.00

Sproson Barrable 1998

Ion

notting hill/west london

Sproson Barrable 1998

Elbow Room

This place has the kind of rugged seductiveness not usually associated with new London bars. Attend in the middle of the afternoon as if you've just left that two-timin' love-of-your-life in bed back at the trailer park and you're trying to decide which town to hit next. Your cool exterior, however, does not hide the turmoil within as you serenely pocket ball after ball and then suddenly miss an easy one. Wrinkle up a sweet smile and have another cold beer.

Never mind this is just Westbourne Grove, home of Planet Organic with Whiteley's and Marks & Spencer just around the corner. So what if the half the guys here are wearing suits and expensive trainers and the girls don't look anything like Sissy Spacek. This place is rockin'.

The designer describes it as 'industrial baroque'. There are worn floorboards of oak and walnut, giant welded-steel, funnel-shaped lights – imagine them swinging wildly if/when a fight should break out – and slightly sleazy purple pool-table tops. The unusual wall finish is a mix of cement, plaster and dye. Bar stools are made of bent curved-steel tubing; wooden tables and ledges for drinks and snacks conveniently hang from every available wall space. The seating has wooden (Norwegian spruce) back panels with chainsaw grooves which look like the work of a madman. The ceiling is carpaint-sprayed black. The loos are marked with pool balls arranged to form his and hers genitalia. Yes groan, but be grateful there are no ropey topless waitresses or exposed lummox beer guts on show.

ADDRESS 103 Westbourne Grove, London W2 (020 7221 5211)
CLIENT Arthur Baker and The Elbow Room Shareholders Company Ltd
UNDERGROUND Bayswater, Notting Hill Gate
OPEN Monday to Saturday, 12.00–23.00; Sunday, 12.00–22.30

Paul Daly 1994

Elbow Room

notting hill/west london

Paul Daly 1994

Liquid Lounge

A simple and comfortable design for a bar. Anything simpler might be boring. The dark wood floor contrasts nicely with the teal blues. Not really that loungey despite the name. There is nowhere to slouch or get remotely horizontal, especially when the bar is busy. Egyptian blue, white-piped booths provide seating for groups (does the person furthest in never have to buy a round?). The red square bar in the centre provides a lot of leaning space as you try to catch the bartender's eye. The strip mirrors everywhere mean you might get lucky and catch someone else's. The outside could be a sleepy South American bar, though not a particularly famous one. Cute slightly retro-shaped pendant lights hang in pairs and cartoony fish-outline artwork hangs on the wall. Stools and bar space against the windows are meant for people looking out but the view is generally uninspiring. Could stay for a while, but only if your friends show up.

ADDRESS 209 Westbourne Grove, London W11 (020 7243 0914)
CLIENT Mark Harris
UNDERGROUND Ladbroke Grove
OPEN Monday to Friday, 17.00–24.00; Saturday, 10.00–24.00; Sunday, 10.00–23.30

Mark Harris and Phillip Wright 1997

Liquid Lounge

notting hill/west london

Mark Harris and Phillip Wright 1997

Jac's

There is something 1960s about the decor here – not a slick *Barbarella* space-capsule fantasy 1960s but more a *Performance*-like one. It is a loosely-scripted space – with a decadent and deliciously soiled sleaze – and one in a perpetual yet fetching state of *déshabille*. The ordinary 1930s façade sports a rusty cut-out steel sign and a large, slightly grotesque, bulbous steel shape with shrivelled tentacles that looks like a dead flower. Inside, the deep maroon walls have framed shelves of books, sculptures and paintings which despite being individually spot-lit are also bathed in the unnatural watery glow from the over-sized fish tank at the centre of the bar. This is the study of an intellectual yet alcoholic old uncle – one who was driven to drink not only by his fierce genius but also its coupling with perhaps unrequited debauched yearnings as, upon close inspection, the artwork depicts tacky naked dancing nymphs and the back room has further dubious murals of entwined couples melding into purple tree-laden landscapes.

Also upon closer inspection, the library is fake, the furniture is mysteriously covered in gold and red velvet and there is not much going on besides drinking. To further add to this dream sequence of a bar is the easily missable – was it there before the stiff drinks? – and impossibly high void above the low group of sofas near the entrance. Here you will find a neck-straining view of windows and balustraded openings but a substantially well-lubricated imagination is necessary to work out what is really up there.

ADDRESS 48 Lonsdale Road, London W11 (020 7792 2838)
UNDERGROUND Ladbroke Grove, Notting Hill Gate
OPEN Monday to Saturday, 18.00–23.00; Sunday, 19.00–22.30

Jasper Gorst and Curtis Saint Clemence 1996

Jasper Gorst and Curtis Saint Clemence 1996

Beach Blanket Babylon

As the name suggests, this bar will provide a venue only for the playful harmless kind of debauchery as opposed to the true leave-town, change-your-name, only-carry-cash-in-small-denominations illegal variety. This has an eclectic jumble-sale mix of textures made of bits of coloured glass, glazed tile, stone, velvet, plastic, terrazzo, wrought iron and rusty steel. Upright curlicued chairs and checkerboard tables at the front give way to more horizontal seating around the side and towards the back where a series of indoor-outdoor spaces is filled with Gaudiesque curves and snuggly JBFed-in-looking corners. With its slightly rumpled air, it feels as if it could just as easily be the home of a beaded soothsayer or well-meaning alternative-medicine quackery involving hard-to-pronounce herbs and tadpole tails.

ADDRESS 45 Ledbury Road, London W11 (020 7229 2907)
CLIENT Robert Newmart
UNDERGROUND Notting Hill Gate
OPEN Monday to Saturday, 11.30–23.00; Sunday, 10.30–22.30 (happy hour Monday to Saturday, 16 .00–20.00; Sunday 12.00–22.30)

Tony Weller 1990

Beach Blanket Babylon

notting hill/west london

Tony Weller 1990

Shadow Bar (at The Hempel)

It is difficult to distinguish the entrance of the hotel from the other buildings on the street, the only clue being a discreet black-on-black letter H on the doormat. Enter through a small still room with an expensive-looking field of potted white orchids into a wide and startlingly bleached-out space. At either end, two symmetrically placed seating areas are formed by a shallow sunken step down and warmed by the slender line of small flames created by a gas fire in the detail-less shelf openings.

Slip past the hotel staff to the right where another white room-like space displays a large dark rectilinear spiral wooden sculpture. This is in fact the stairwell down to the bar. The steps are exceptionally thick slabs of textured semi-opaque Perspex which feels both substantial and light. Entering the bar from the side, a distinct lack of bar fixtures and clutter leaves you momentarily disoriented and unsure of your destination. You have, however, just found the perfect place to detox your mind with intoxicating liquids. The small yet surprisingly uncramped space is sandwiched between an extremely high aluminium bar front and two floor-to-ceiling etched-glass screens. These form the backing for the square, black-wood bench and stools whose nod to comfort comes in the form of smooth black cotton padded seats. Pale back-lit side walls have a single horizontal shelf cut into them where three black cups (with metallic insides) have been carefully placed on the black surface. Strangely, no one seems to be using these. Other considered placements include the row of wooden vessels arranged according to size – apparently symbolising richness – behind the bar below square aluminium box cupboards; the symmetrical display of bunches of papyrus shoots; and the rhythmic positioning of slate place mats on the long central table. No salted peanuts here – help yourself instead to a decorative selection of pumpkin seeds, sweet cashews or curried, cinnamoned slices of dried

Anoushka Hempel 1996

Shadow Bar (at The Hempel)

Anoushka Hempel 1996

apple from the swivelling tiers of square black nut bowls.

The wide gap running clear through the centre of the bar and into the dining area is meant to be a strip of positive energy flowing through the space and it is with the utmost seriousness that staff obey the rule which forbids them to walk through it. The five elements of fire, water, steel, wood and earth provide the theme used in the choice of materials.

On your way out, as you float once again past reception do not miss looking up into the huge multi-storey void. The vaulted ceiling is impossibly and breathtakingly high and the large projected black and white film-star image instills this otherwise spartan atmosphere with a whiff of decadent glamour and welcome frivolity.

ADDRESS 31–35 Craven Hill Gardens, London W2 (020 7298 9000)
UNDERGROUND Lancaster Gate, Queensway, Bayswater
OPEN 11.00–23.00 (residents only)

Anoushka Hempel 1996

Shadow Bar (at The Hempel)

Anoushka Hempel 1996

fulham/kensington

Fluid

A delightful capsule of a bar despite one serious drawback – no alcoholic fluids. But at least you're not the designated driver and the ONLY person in the room not drinking. Everyone here is merely combining fruits.

From across the road the Fluid shopfront with its blueberry sign, large pale tiles and glowing interior seems a refreshing promise of something special. It is like an open fridge door on a hot summer evening while shiny lemon Perspex walls offer a ray of sun on grey days. The detail of the façade tiles making an 'F' whose little arm continues inside to form the smallest of bar tops must make you smile. The space is lit by three recessed wall panels which glow brightly from their edges. A distorted reflection of these can be seen in the opposite wall which displays the clear logo in a font which resembles the way spilt liquid holds its shape by surface tension. Most of the space on the smooth curved-edged wood bar is taken up by three noisy juicers which leave you screaming at your companions when they're switched off. The Dalsouple flooring is the exact colour of the algae/wheatgrass/lawn clippings drink so favoured by supermodels.

Chairs look like the offspring of an Eames LCW crossed with a Jacobsen Ant in IKEA-vitro fertilisation. The yellow moulded-plastic tilted saucer-shape bar stools are a catalogue model which is cropping up everywhere. A teeny row of clear Perspex shelves shows a minuscule selection of Nutri-grain bars. No pork scratchings here.

ADDRESS 208 Fulham Road, London SW10 (020 7352 4372)
CLIENT Tim Scott
UNDERGROUND South Kensington, Fulham Broadway, Earls Court
OPEN Monday to Friday, 7.30-21.00, Saturday, 9.00-21.00

Misha Stefan 1999

Fluid

Misha Stefan 1999

Cactus Blue

Terracotta, Navaho rugs, stylised rattlesnake images, battered bits of copper and tin – we all remember the symptoms of a particular home-decor virus which swept through many residential habitats on this, but especially on the other side of the Atlantic, briefly bringing everything else near to extinction. Widely referred to as the Sante Fé look, it had a run of a good few years then mysteriously disappeared. And now here it is, in all its glory, replicating in a Fulham bar. In the rapidly changing world of bar design, when a certain style has a brief respite its reappearance will immediately be dubbed retro. This speaks of a neurotic need to hide the fact that one's bar is not exactly cutting edge but, horror of horrors, lagging behind from a past trend. The logical step is to stake a claim as the first or the quickest to revive.

In any case, the timing of this bar's theme makes it a bit of a maverick – *avant* or otherwise. Desperately trying to set some kind of atmosphere, south-western (United States) motifs jostling for attention include plenty of knackered-looking cacti (none of which looks too happy with its adopted locale); colourful Mexican tilework; a rather ugly striped and zig-zagged composition of black and yellow tiles on the ceiling (Navaho blanket patterns do not translate well into glossy standard tile work); perforated copper shelves behind the bar; and supposedly sun-bleached patchy paintwork of burnt yellows, terracottas and blue-greens. The springy bar stools add a welcome and appropriate bit of comic cartoon tension (did they arrive in a big box marked ACME?) while the bar front is playfully wrapped in a metallic fishscale pattern topped by still more copper.

The ceiling of the main space has been knocked through to create a mezzanine level, in the middle of which hangs an impressively large chandelier from whose curlicued arms dangle bits of colourful glass. The

Brian Stein 1996

Cactus Blue

fulham/kensington

Brian Stein 1996

mechanised tray which travels between the levels has been adapted from a yacht's mast.

Although many of the details are tired clichés and seem a bit false, the actual scale and volume of the space do remind one of a saloon bar *circa* frontier time – if only as featured in a Hollywood western. With a bit of imagination, one could choreograph that classic scene here – a chair-smashing brawl breaks out after a stuntman drops dramatically and directly on to the bar as a woman of ill-repute wearing a frilly yellow dress rushes to grasp the balustrade above and lets out a husky scream. Cut. Indeed, the industrial-looking structure to the added staircase does look as if it could support a massive film crew and camera. Oh … all of a sudden we've got ourselves an atmosphere.

ADDRESS 86 Fulham Road, London SW3 (020 7823 7858)
CLIENT Brian Stein
UNDERGROUND South Kensington
OPEN Monday to Friday, 17.30–23.30, Saturday and Sunday, 12.00–23.00 (happy hour 17.30–19.30)

Cactus Blue

fulham/kensington

Brian Stein 1996

itsu

An artfully designed brochure has an accompanying manifesto that has the pseudo-casual yet annoyingly selfish tone of a spoiled brat – almost every sentence begins with 'I want …' – which presumably is how they perceive their punters. It claims to want, among other things, 'the freedom to go when I want, with whom I want, at any time convenient to me'. Strange then, that when I visited itsu early one evening (just past five) the bar staff announced that no drinks could be served until five thirty: 'You can want all you like, you're not getting a drink.'

The layout of this first-floor bar is divided into two main seating areas. The first, at the front, has deep banquettes below dark wood-screened windows. Scattered red and orange pillows look too carefully arranged to be mussed up by anyone wishing to sink into them. At the rear of the space, below a skylight also covered in dark wood screening, is another low L-shaped banquette area, similar to the other except the pillows are in various tones of gold and burnt ochre. An old knee-height wooden table undoubtedly crafted somewhere in south-east Asia means one has to hunch over, perched on the edge of the seat, to reach drinks. The curved pieces which cover the wall lighting above the bar look like lanterns and give the room a sensuous yellow glow. A golden-yellow textured fabric lines the wall. The two seating areas are joined by the thinnest of corridors with built-in, single-file, dark-wood, bar-height stools, upholstered in Chinese reds, and matching tables along its length. Their stilt-like appearance make them look precarious and uninviting despite the proximity of an accompanying shoulder-height magazine rack. Lest we forget though, this bar is located in an area where women who shop in stilettoed mules can race after cabs with alarming vigour and speed.

Mediocre Chinese scroll paintings and pottery adorn the nooks and crannies and Japanese newspapers have been varnished on to the walls

Wolff Olins 1999 (refurbishment)

Wolff Olins 1999 (refurbishment)

of the loos. The use of type in a foreign language regardless of its content has always seemed a bit dubious – *vice-versa* examples (foreign beers called 'Sweat' or Continental youths wearing T-shirts emblazoned with 'bum' or 'sissy') are easy laughs.

The concept obviously aims for sultry exoticism but the actual arrangement with its pervading air of clinical tidiness make it unclear whether this is a venue where one is supposed to languish with a drink or sit impossibly upright with the weighty austerity and discipline normally reserved for Japanese tea ceremonies.

ADDRESS 118 Draycott Avenue, London SW3 (020 7584 5522)
UNDERGROUND South Kensington
OPEN Monday to Saturday, 18.00–24.00

Wolff Olins 1999 (refurbishment)

itsu

fulham/kensington

Wolff Olins 1999 (refurbishment)

8.12

Putney Bridge

As there are precious few opportunities to drink by the river, it is with much regret that one finds – having come all the way to Putney and laying down West End prices for a couple of drinks – the view of the Thames at sofa-eye-level totally obscured. The original interior, fitted-out at the time of the building's construction two years ago, was a mainly monochrome affair with decked wood and some nautical touches – and served primarily as a temporary anchorage for those waiting to dine upstairs. The refurb was commissioned to make the bar a worthy destination in its own right and, although you cannot see the murky Thames from a sitting position, you can still appreciate the equally rare sight of an unobstructed expanse of London sky.

The entrance has been brought forward to create a dramatic approach to this long and narrow ground-floor space. The lighting and mood change immediately as you pass under the cream spiral stairs. It now seems to glow various shades of blues and purples. The ceiling is painted an off-white blue; the dark purple fabric-covered lampshades cast a lavender hue on the surroundings, and the strong cobalt-blue crackle-glazed bar top (pyra lava) reflects against the mirrored back wall of watery aquamarine shapes. The actual bar is shaped like a Kellogg's 'K' and faced in an aubergine marble plaster finish. Walls are panelled in alternating horizontally and vertically striped squares of Zebrano wood which gives it the slightly kitsch appearance of a suburban American basement home bar. Furniture is a collection of specially made chairs and sofas in textured indigo-blue fabric and brown leather, and small chrome-edged coffee tables with striped walnut and oak veneer. These come in 'L' shaped pairs which slot together satisfyingly.

Even deeper into the space, a few more seats and tables are lit by large

David Collins 1999 (refurbishment)

Putney Bridge

David Collins 1999 (refurbishment)

square doughnut wall-lights made of yellowed parchment glued on to Perspex. A sunken area – enclosed by glass walls with tree patterns that mimic the real silhouettes outside – is filled with groups of sofas, presumably for marginally more (look but don't touch) private parties.

ADDRESS Lower Richmond Road, London SW15 (020 8780 1811)
UNDERGROUND Putney Bridge
OPEN Monday to Friday, 11.30–23.00; Saturday, 11.30–23.00; Sunday, 11.30–22.30

David Collins 1999 (refurbishment)

RCA Art Bar

Good to see a minimal space using a saturated colour instead of white. Everything is red: the walls, the vinyl of the bench seating and stools (whose legs are also red), and the shiny red bar itself. A simple neon sign marks the entrance. Tables are plain white Corian squares. The large logo on the floor looks as if the font has been laboured over. Pendant lights are made from Beck's bottles and ashtrays are made from the unused bottom bits. Nothing is wasted in this bar except the … a pun could be made here. Stylised trees of acid green serve as coat racks. They look as if they have grown through the small circular bar-height tables and will continue to grow through the ceiling. The boxed bottles of Beck's above the bar are meant to display the sponsor's logo in the same enigmatic way as much contemporary advertising – you have to work at it, the logic being that this forced engagement with the brand will make it more memorable. Whatever the case, the design exudes a certain self-conscious cockiness which is sure to appeal to future patrons and clients.

ADDRESS Royal College of Art, Kensington Gore, London SW7 (020 7590 4444)
CLIENT RCA Students' Union
UNDERGROUND South Kensington
OPEN not open to the public; you have to be taken in by an RCA student

Gitta Gschwendtner and Angel Monzon 1998

RCA Art Bar

Gitta Gschwendtner and Angel Monzon 1998

Crescent

This bar is not ugly, which is unfortunate. Indifference, we have learnt over the years, is sometimes worse than hate – and in this case, a tangible ugliness would at least have made this place memorable. The atmosphere is so tame that even a slew of gimmicks – say fifteen people balanced on a swiftly passing bicycle or a wild beast roaming the aisle between the bar and tables – would not have much of an impact.

Plywood chairs and dark wood-stained surfaces are meant to set off the purple upholstered banquette which runs the length of the space. The continuous wooden rack mounted on the wall above reminds one of a passenger-train's overhead shelf, except of course this isn't going anywhere. Behind the bar, steel-box shelves neatly encase each bottle, giving the space some *more* order. The back wall is painted an annoying camouflage pattern in tasteful muted lavenders, matched with milky insipid weak-tea beiges and mousey browns. A once-popular street-fashion motif has been taken from its functional army/utility source and filtered through the high street, through the designer shops and back again to appear on this wall, completely drained of any pertinence.

The base of the bar has a ribbed wooden surface along which one can run one's bored fingers to make a satisfying 'thud, thud, thud'. This bar is not completely useless – it's a perfect venue in which to rehearse such personal skills as – for instance – staring into space without blinking.

ADDRESS 99 Fulham Road, London SW3 (020 7225 2244)
CLIENT Paul Medhurst
UNDERGROUND South Kensington
OPEN Monday to Friday, 11.00–23.30; Saturday, 10.00–23.30; Sunday, 11.00–22.30

BOA (Ed Barber and Jay Osgerby) 1996

BOA (Ed Barber and Jay Osgerby) 1996

south london/south bank

Brixtonian Havana Club

Judging by the characterless alley in which this bar is located, you can safely assume that it is not relying on any passing trade. It does enhance the feeling that it's some kind of 'find' or that you are somehow in the know for going there – always a plus in a bar. The door, a few steps above street level, leads to a steep flight of stairs whose ascent takes just long enough for you to start wondering whose idea it was to come here in the first place.

It's all right when you get here though! Originally a warehouse of some sort, the space has had a variety of uses including restaurant and health-food shop. It has an impressively high pitched ceiling with exposed rafters and skylights. Besides the bottles and bottles of rum sitting behind the bar, the first things that attract your panning gaze are the colourful blobs of pink, red, and baby blues which form the panels of the bar and the partition around the opposite stairwell. These are made by sandwiching large drops of resin between sheets of Perspex; the result looks like a frozen version of yesterday's plaything, the Lava Lamp. The panels look as if they taste sweet which is a good thing when one discovers the theme of the rest of the decor. Owner Vincent Osborne has taken it upon himself to interpret the dark voodoo religion of Santameria as a theme for the bar. This is the source and explanation behind the large gilt mirror and painting of Shango, keeper of the gate and god of iron and strength, which peeps out from behind the blobbed screens. The white vein markings on the floor are also to do with Santamerian symbols which Osborne reassuringly claims are only to do with love and harmony. It is a relief to hear that the voodoo aspects would never work as 'we haven't put blood down or made any sacrifices and that sort of thing'.

The bar top is made of wenge, a dark African hardwood, marked at intervals with an attractive striped and aptly named wood called Zebrano

Peter Vetter, Marcel Weidner and Vincent Osborne 1999

Brixtonian Havana Club

Peter Vetter, Marcel Weidner and Vincent Osborne 1999

which is also used to edge the gold panels of the behind-the-bar shelves. Ant chairs are repainted red and white to match the simple circular tables. The bench seating in the inner room has soft red-leather backing which licks the walls like the flames of a fire. Convoluted steel shapes designed by a friend of the owner form vases and some subsidiary lighting fixtures. Downstairs, the loos are sponsored by Absolut Vodka and are made of see-through coloured Perspex with Absolut labels embedded in the toilet-seat covers.

The space is actually rather awkwardly divided by the boxed-in glass-brick lobby which looks Cuban only in a purple Lycra, Miami-Sound-Machine kind of way, an enclosed office bricked-in above the inner room, and a strange mezzanine with a wooden balustrade at the other end. But this clumsiness in layout is completely overshadowed by the over-riding personality of the space. There is a great sense of fun and flourish and skewed inventiveness about the details which must come from the enjoyment with which this place was obviously designed.

ADDRESS 11 Beehive Place, London SW9 (020 7924 9262)
CLIENT Vincent Osborne
UNDERGROUND Brixton
OPEN Tuesday and Wednesday, 12.00–1.00; Thursday to Saturday, 12.00–2.00

Brixtonian Havana Club

Peter Vetter, Marcel Weidner and Vincent Osborne 1999

Tuba

A blatant matt-silver tube logo which tops the curved glass façade signals this unusually creative capsule space. Huge, glowing, egg-white flexible plastic pods look eerily sci-fi and hang from the ceiling as if ready to burst with alien life. Bar lighting is also creature-like, as thin segmented limbs of pivoting steel parts culminate in tiny heads which light the clear rolled-up plastic menus. The direct route through this narrow space has horizontal wood-board flooring which feels like a gangplank for this jokey comic-book spaceship. Walls and columns are a playful mint green and bright yellow. Chairs look sweet and edible in plain and orange clear plastic and gaufrette-shaped tables are a smooth, pale wood. The checkerboard floor warps into a curve reminiscent of graphics representing space as it goes into a black hole. From across the street it looks as if the logo is actually a strong rod of steel which has been forcefully rammed between the neighbouring shopfronts in order to squeeze out this jolly little drinking place.

ADDRESS 4 Clapham Common Southside, London SW4 (020 7978 3333)
CLIENT Adriano Monachello
UNDERGROUND Clapham Common
OPEN Tuesday to Thursday, 11.00–24.00; Friday and Saturday, 11.00–1.00; Sunday, 12.00–24.00

anand zenz 1998

Tuba

south london/south bank

anand zenz 1998

Bar Room Bar

Pleasant, pleasant, pleasant. This bright, sunny, airy, high-ceilinged, large-windowed space is refreshing in its lack of aspiration to be cool – which, come to think of it, is really the epitome of coolness itself. This is not to say insufficient effort has gone into the design process. The feel is easy-going rather than lazy. Bar staff seem unafraid to smile. Ungaudy yet vibrant tones of yellow, green, and ... aubergine, paprika and pumpkin stripe the walls. Solid boxy shelves behind the bar support the selection of bottles, considerately lit from beneath to cut glare.

The spaciousness of the bar allows for a good number of tables and an uncramped arrangement of clean leather (not vintage) sofas in navy, butterscotch and caramel. Chairs are upholstered in a bouclé fabric reminiscent of the material of those little boxy suits worn – with matching hats and a string of pearls – by women in the early 1960s. The curved wooden bar bellows out away from a protruding corner to form a roomy behind-the-bar area. The fluid form is echoed in a cream false-ceiling panel and in the black lacquered wood and stone flooring. Fun lighting includes a row of chandeliers made of glass cups and a fat fibre-optic wall light which looks like a plate of chubby spaghetti. A large outdoor space at the back is partially covered by a wide blue-striped awning. The only disappointing feature is the framed artwork on the walls which looks Athena-bought – cosmetic rather than inspiring. Altogether a calm and winsome space in which to enjoy a drink.

(There's another branch of Bar Room Bar at 48 Rosslyn Hill, London NW3; 020 7435 0808.)

ADDRESS 441 Battersea Park Road, London SW8 (020 7223 7721)
RAIL Clapham Junction, Battersea Park
OPEN Monday to Saturday, 11.00–23.00; Sunday, 11.00–22.00

Bistrot 2

Second-floor neighbour of the More Flamboyant One upstairs (see page 9.12), this is altogether a less uptight affair, probably because it knows it can never compete as they share a selling point – the view – and this will always rate an unchangeble 2:8. Let's face it, no one visits a 'tower' to stick around on the second floor. The layout is simple and maximises the panorama by backing the 15-metre-long bar against the opposite wall, leaving no seat far from the large windows. Light wood floorboards and the primary-coloured square columns which divide the groups of matching Ant chairs look vaguely 1980s in a Scandinavian or Dutch way. The bar itself is a continuous wave of aqua blue light and contrasts nicely with the millions of little twinkles emanating from across the Thames.

ADDRESS Riverside, Oxo Tower Wharf, Barge House Street, London SE1 (020 7401 8200)
UNDERGROUND Waterloo
OPEN Monday to Saturday, 12.00–23.00; Sunday, 11.30–18.00

Apicella Associates 1996

Bistrot 2

Apicella Associates 1996

Oxo Tower

This is the tastefully unstylish home of the £7.50 cocktail where one would expect the prices at least to guarantee access to the only known view to allow London a skyline. Elevators open out to face south London, whetting the appetite for the more impressive anticipated view of St Paul's and The Temple. However, when bar is chosen over brasserie, you are immediately shown the corridor which leads past the centrally placed loos to a unremarkable corner area with supermarket-new brick walls. You buy a drink and carefully work your way around to the windows to soak in the view and alcohol. You then bump into the grand piano and the realisation hits you – no view! Unless you buy a meal (or perhaps several in order to build up a perception of loyalty), access is blocked.

The back-seat choices left are: up against the leather bar in an 1980s shade of blue, perched on surprisingly attractive brushed-steel bar stools whose seats look appealingly soft like a succulent leaf; or do a complete about-face and sit in the lower Bertoia chairs from where your view is not even a neck-strain away and shift your attention to your companions. It is even difficult to appreciate the newly added high-tech aerofoil roof from this space; the protruding cantilevered structure is undramatically foreshortened from the inside. It would be a far better experience to drink from a beer can on the opposite bank of the Thames and look back at the roof and the glowing letters of the Oxo tower since this was the original intention anyway. Has this bar ever had a repeat visit?

ADDRESS Riverside, Oxo Tower Wharf, Barge House Street, London SE1 (020 7803 3888)
CLIENT Harvey Nichols Restaurants Ltd
UNDERGROUND Waterloo
OPEN Monday to Saturday, 11.00–23.00; Sunday, 11.00–22.00

Lifschutz Davidson 1996

Lifschutz Davidson 1996

north london

Bierodrome

Two-hundred beer bottles have been suspended in a dark amber resin which is backlit to form an elegant wordless alternative signpost for this new Islington version of a Belgian beer hall. The 1930s façade of this ex-local-council neighbourhood office, once painted bright pink and white, is now in 'Lizard Green', one of the signature Belgo paint colours originally developed by Quentin Reynolds (see R K Stanley, page 2.52) for the first of the Belgo restaurants.

This space shows an excellent integration of graphics and architecture with the blown-up image of a Belgian couple taken from a postcard providing another non-verbal example of house branding. The double barrels, forming a recumbent letter B, are meant to differentiate between a darker (panelled) drinking area (why is drinking always the 'darker' pursuit?) and the lighter (rendered) dining area. The drinking/dining ratio of 7:3 has unfortunately been overestimated and diners worm their way round the back to occupy the rear part of the vaulted oak-veneer panelled tunnel. The area is separated by a curtain in the same soft dark-brown leather as the waitresses' aprons.

The simple square furniture has been given a dark Jacobean oak finish to match the segment of horizontal tubular rolls of leather which form banquettes reminiscent of Eileen Gray's Bibendum chair. Cut-out windows look into the glass-backed Snapps fridge which caters to those strange few who come to a place called Bierodrome intending to drink something other than beer. Backlit Reglit screens, a popular industrial material used in France and the Netherlands in the 1960s, are used to build up a back wall, with a front wall holding the curious 201st suspended beer bottle. This is apparently the number of different kinds of beers available, which the majority disturbingly avoids in favour of Stella Artois. This selection has meant that a vast area and system were

Tony Sayer (Tim Bush Associates) and Denis Blaies 1999

Bierodrome

Tony Sayer (Tim Bush Associates) and Denis Blaies 1999

needed to store the 201 different kinds of glasses.

A minimal concrete fireplace reinforces the ski-lodge/ beer-hall image. Other plain elements which replace the usual cutesy naff alpine clutter of real chalets are the single bent-steel piece which forms a menu/magazine rack, the lacquered, bright mild-steel chandelier ring of horizontal lightbulbs and the unusual 'antique' finish to the zinc sheets which clad the bar front.

ADDRESS 173–174 Upper Street, London N1 (020 7226 5835)
CLIENT Belgo Ltd
UNDERGROUND Angel, Highbury and Islington
OPEN Monday to Sunday, 12.00–23.00

Tony Sayer (Tim Bush Associates) and Denis Blaies 1999

Bierodrome

Tony Sayer (Tim Bush Associates) and Denis Blaies 1999

WKD

The most engaging aspect of this bar design is actually visible from a speeding car. The two-storey glass-fronted façade, broken up by huge purple banners bearing the bar's name, reveals a ground-floor and mezzanine space in which one can just about make out some angled walls and bar areas to the left on both floors. All attention is drawn towards the huge tubular lantern lights which fill the double-height space in the front. These look like giant fluorescent tubes in pink, purple, yellow and cyan. Each tube has a different repetitive pattern of either goldfish, strawberries, pale blue budgies or daisies. These appear so bright and funky that the actual interior is bound to disappoint.

The bar is in desperate need of a refurb but one can only see the odd – and sadly ineffectual – little added touch such as a strange plantless wall planter and a row of makeshift mirrored tiles. These efforts seem wistful, as if recognising the much bigger potential of the space. A motorised lighting mechanism – projecting a variety of swirling shapes on to the floor and walls – which is attached to the ceiling looks high-tech, expensive and out of place. The animated bar staff give the place a dose of personality which is wasted on the unworthy and despondent decor.

Keep driving into Grimshaw's Sainsbury's, buy some cheap party favours, stock up on some booze and make your own funky bar in the living room when you get home – not half as sad.

ADDRESS 18 Kentish Town Road, London NW1 (020 7267 1869)
UNDERGROUND Camden Town
OPEN Monday to Thursday, 12.00–2.00; Friday, Saturday, 12.00–3.00; Sunday, 12.00–1.00

various owners and staff 1991

various owners and staff 1991

Embassy Bar

This split wedge-shaped space has been given just the right amount of a makeover – too little and it would have looked a tad run down, perhaps a bit dated and not so special; too much and it would have lost that comfy worn-in feel and perhaps start looking serious, stiff and not so special. From the outside, with its dark-blue-painted brick exterior and etched rectangular patterns on the windows, it looks as if the interior fit-out might be predictably decked out with Italian designer lounge seats or perhaps a study in bare-faced concrete and stainless steel. Fortunately, its few new additions blend gracefully in with the old.

Enormous double black-and-white David Bailey portraits of Michael Caine circa *Alfie* grace either side of the space and you feel as if just a bit of the swinging hipness of that era might rub off on to the evening. At the same time there is a vaguely North-American feel – perhaps because there bars are sometimes allowed to coast for decades without a refit, without having to keep up, and often steadily build up layers and layers of character.

The wood parquet flooring has the unusual staggered pattern of a brick wall. The ceiling is strangely segmented into radiating parts and all mouldings and architraves are dark brown ribbed wood.

Old built-in red-leather booth seats run all the way along the walls, separated by small U-shaped wooden tables whose sides are painted mint green. The chairs grouped around these also have old red-leather upholstery and either tiny circular or curved rectangular backs. These are low and friendly and near the entrance, while further back at the two ends of the rooms there are woodgrain-look Formica tables in various boomerang, kidney and artist's-palette shapes. These have funny little mint-green shaded lights which look odd but good, and contrast well with the old orange-coloured split-cylinder wall lamps.

details unknowable

Embassy Bar

details unknowable

Embassy Bar

The curved central bar has the personality of an old car. Its dark wooden top has a separated handrail running along its edge – which feels so good in the hand you hesitate before letting go. Below this is a steel-edged teal-blue Formica front with a small shelf tucked in between. The steel-capped wooden footrest looks worn but strong. Behind the bar a patch of black mosaic interspersed with gold together with the black steel-rimmed overhead lighting fixture speak of a more luxurious past. If this bar were a person he would be wise and tired but completely on the ball.

ADDRESS 119 Essex Road, London N1
UNDERGROUND Angel
OPEN Monday to Thursday, 17.00–23.00; Friday and Saturday, 17.00–1.00; Sunday, 15.00–22.30

Embassy Bar

north london

details unknowable

Cube Bar

A curious location for a bar – this part of Finchley Road is normally associated with anxious thoughts of aggressively weaving traffic and multiple lane changes. These are often accompanied by furtive glances at neighbouring cars and, motivated by self-preservation, quick assessments (telltale signs are clenched teeth, a red face or the murderous yet strangely serene cold-blooded stare) to check the psychological fitness of those behind the wheel. Applying both standard and some highly original examples of sign language – sorrys, pardon-mes and thank-you-kindlys – one usually tries to accelerate off into the night as soon as possible, grateful just to get out of the area.

But sometimes a local friend will insist and you will remember a vague neon sign in the midst of all that drama. The Cube Bar is in fact a highly original and appropriate space for a bar. Located on three floors of a former Barclay's Bank, the modernity of the original early 1960s development – ten floors of housing over offices, above the articulated structures of shops and bank – exudes a powerful nostalgia for the ideals of the architecture of that era, made all the more poignant by the profession's present ineffectual state. One almost feels an urge to party here, just to prove something to the planners of 30 years ago.

The blue cathode graphics are reminiscent of the work of light artists from the late 1960s and early 1970s. Bronze letters have been removed from the façade and replaced by two lines which mimic a crossed cheque, leaving only the aptly descriptive 'BAR'. The large plate-glass window above has a sculptural bronze frame and modern tapered detail which lines up with the pendant lights inside. This reveals both the double-height space of the ground-floor bar and the mezzanine above.

The entrance is a heavy-looking door/wall which slides along the façade to reveal the tiled room-like space of the wide-staired entrance

Madigan & Donald originally, but refurbished 1999

Cube Bar

Madigan & Donald originally, but refurbished 1999

lobby. A layer of lacquered birch-faced plywood panels floats away from the original walls and strategically placed cut-outs are made for the handrail and concealed lighting. The main bar has a perforated aluminium front and the beauty of Finchley Road behind. A lift shaft at the rear of the space has been removed and replaced by stairs with a missing ceiling panel to reveal the lift-cable wheels and mechanism. Doors have tiny windows the same size and shape as the handguard. After a while the repetitive theme of moving and missing panels leaves one wondering whether they all slide back or open to reward the curious-minded.

In 1999 the bar was given the Shaun Clarkson purple treatment. Ant chairs and other moulded plywood seats and tables have been replaced by purple-padded, upholstered boxes and padded banquettes – the owners have obviously been sold the 'lounge' word. On the first floor, sad net curtains have been fitted which unfortunately hide the interesting collection of rectangular windows at varying heights – one can only guess that they've been sold the 'boudoir' word as well.

ADDRESS 135 Finchley Road, London NW3 (020 7483 2393)
CLIENT The Mean Fiddler
UNDERGROUND Swiss Cottage
OPEN Monday to Thursday, 17.00–24.00; Friday and Saturday, 17.00–24.30; Sunday, 17.00–23.30

Madigan & Donald originally, but refurbished 1999

Madigan & Donald originally, but refurbished 1999

Bartok

This is a soothing architecture, immediately appealing to all the senses as you push past the large, dark, veneered door and slip in. The music of the live quartet appears to come from behind as you glide with outstretched arms towards the bar. You haven't realised it yet, but this is what you've been searching for all your life – or all night anyway – somewhere to rest your weary head and please make that a double so I don't have to get up too soon.

Dive in slow motion on to the low squarish bilberry-coloured sofa that lines the length of the room. A cool blue glow emanates from the cluster of rectangular lightboxes on the wall. Those who profess to provide chill-out zones are legion, yet here's the real thing, well off the beaten crawl. Chalk Farm – who would have thought it?

The site was formerly a pub with a corner entrance. This was moved around to the side to make way for the impressively large windows, directly in front of which sits the quartet – hence the feeling of music washing over you when you stand at the bar. The bar itself is topped in a dark-midnight terrazzo with smooth, pale, chunky aggregates which, together with the retro-looking Brasilia espresso machine, feel vaguely of another time or place. In fact, this is exactly what it is – there is an over-riding feeling of displacement here. The kind of sensation you get on your first night out abroad and you feel lightheaded but not exactly tired as you wonder what time it is back home. A lack of an easy familiarity with the surroundings is coupled with odd instances of recognition. The shop-spray painted MDF box frames for the lights, which look deceivingly like Bakelite or ceramic, are similar to those found in Denim (see page 2.16). You saw the vintage gilt-framed blackboards in Jerusalem (see page 2.40), and the cast-resin door handle and plush square-doughnut stools all trigger memories. These are the signature details of the designer

Shaun Clarkson 1999

Shaun Clarkson 1999

Bartok

Shaun Clarkson. At Bartok the context feels very different. Perhaps it is the intimate size of the space without the usual crowd that makes it feel less London-like. There is a hyperness that is missing and welcomely so.

When you do choose to focus your attention (no hurry) you can see that the details are equally divided between the classical and the modern – a pairing which works extremely well in this instance. For example, two of the columns are original and ornate but a third, assimilating nicely, is simple, square-cut and devoid of ornamentation. Older library chairs upholstered in new but traditional materials sit comfortably with the contemporary-looking chenille-bouclé sofas. Stop focusing though and let the surroundings seep into your subconscious – a veritable palliative to the discord of the rest of the night.

ADDRESS 78–79 Chalk Farm Road, London NW1 (020 7916 0595)
CLIENT The Mean Fiddler
UNDERGROUND Chalk Farm
OPEN Monday to Friday, 17.00–23.00; Saturday, 11.00–23.00; Sunday, 12.00–22.30 (happy hour Monday to Friday, 17.00–19.00)

Shaun Clarkson 1999

Bartok

north london

Shaun Clarkson 1999

Toast

Designers 4IV were previously known for their interiors at Harvey Nichols. This is telling – Toast's cautious elegance is a sort of department-store chic. The finish is clean and smooth but unfortunately falls on the duller side of cutting-edge design. Furniture comprises tastefully selected chairs from Milan and sensible, heavily varnished walnut-veneered tables. A VIP area has a curved wall padded in caramel-coloured leather. The other walls are timidly given a patchy varnished cream finish.

The more interesting bits are hidden behind the matt-black granite bar. The back wall is lined with smoky glass, which joyfully adds a touch of sleaze. Two colourful bunches of curved slim tubular lighting break up the otherwise refined monotony of muted browns and beiges. The best detail is the Ab Fab illuminated champagne sink bearing the bar's logo. This, incidentally, is of an angled top view of a wine glass and resembles a skewed version of the Lucky Strike logo. The sinks in the loo are trying to be special and use a tried and tested sloped draining surface. Not much oomph here but it is certainly likeable and nice.

ADDRESS 50 Hampstead High Street, London NW3 (020 7431 2244)
CLIENT Uri Nachoom
UNDERGROUND Hampstead
OPEN Monday to Sunday, 11.00–24.00

4IV 1999

Scala

Although this is more of a club than a bar, the first floor is open during the day for drink and snacks. It is designed by the multi-disciplinarian acronym of the moment, FAT (Fashion, Architecture, Taste), who are more famous for talking about themselves in clever sound-bites than actual built work. Goal statements such as 'High content culture for the airbag generation' and 'Art for the wealthy and houses for the poor' do engender 'high curiosity' from the middling terminally mortgaged lot whose knowledge of current architecture stems mainly from Sunday colour supplements.

The foyer bar is the part most people remember from the Scala's days as a repertory cinema. The space has been kept simple with the odd classical detail being picked up on and exaggerated. Sofas are placed right up against the wall emphasising its boxed shape, in a stern configuration which must be tongue-in-cheek. The wood panelling to the floor continues up to sill height to form a narrow ledge for bums and drinks. A large window has been knocked through which looks like the window you would draw in a game of Pictionary. This is an odd but pleasant space. The single slogan which wraps around the wall urges you to 'Reclaim your autonomy in the company of enemies'. Yes, but can I finish my pint first?

ADDRESS 275 Pentonville Road, London N1 (020 7833 2022)
CLIENT Shaun MacClusky
UNDERGROUND King's Cross
OPEN Monday to Thursday, 12.00–16.00, 22.00–3.00; Friday and Saturday, 12.00–16.00, 22.00–5.00

FAT 1999

Scala

north london

FAT 1999

index

Index

Index

Index

Index

PICTURES

All photographs are by Keith Collie except:
page 1.8 by Heike Löwenstein
pages 1.19, 1.29, 1.31, 2.15, 2.21, 2.23, 5.7, 6.3, 7.19, 8.3, 10.23 by Juanita Cheung, who also drew the picture at the end of the book

matches: a league table

Matches: a league table

Apologies to those whose matches were a bit too elusive.

SCORE	BAR – comment
10	LAB – a beautiful reason to start smoking
9	CICADA
	KEMIA – great combination of handsome men and colourful heads
	LOBBY BAR – battleship grey matchheads contrast nicely with muddy grey box
	MASH – Hallowe'en colours given new meaning
	OXO TOWER
	POINT 101 – bright, slick and simple
8	AXIS
	BANK – simple, frugal design
	CACTUS BLUE
	CUBE BAR
	GREAT EASTERN DINING ROOM – matchbook doesn't close
	L.E.D.
	MATCH – oh, the pressure to be clever
	SAK – *trompe l'oeil* Dymo
7	CAN BAR – cute
	CHINA WHITE – seductively secretive
	DETROIT
	DUST
	ELBOW ROOM
	FREEDOM – if only the bar interior were as thoughtfully designed

Matches: a league table

HOME

1 LOMBARD STREET

PHARMACY – great marketing technique in action: no.15 in a series of 60

THE SOCIAL – lush

AKA – note strange heads

6 CHE (+ 10) – sometimes size does matter – when it's a cigar

PUTNEY BRIDGE – takes itself too seriously

5 BIERODROME

SAINT

4 CANTALOUPE

COQ D'ARGENT

THE PLAYER – nothing special but captures cheap and sleazy look to which bar interior aspires

ST JOHN

TOAST – points for the logo, not the matchbox

3 BISTROT 2

57 JERMYN STREET – pseudo swank – bonus marks for appropriateness

JAC'S

R K STANLEY

2 BARTOK

BEACH BLANKET BABYLON – ugly as sin

CIRCUS – puzzlingly fussy font

YO BELOW – plastic lighters available instead

1 THE '10' ROOM

0 CRESCENT – uglier than sin

– FLUID – too scared to ask for matches

Lab

Restaurant Familial

mash

OXO

point 101

CACTUS
BLUE

UBE bar

great eastern

matches

SAK.

detroit

DUST

The Elbow Room
103 WESTBOURNE GROVE, LONDON W2 4UW TEL: 0171 221 5211

I

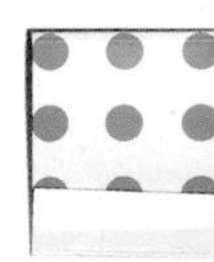

a.k.a.
18 West Central Street
London WC1
Tel. 0171 836 0110
www.the-end.co.uk

che

BIERODROME
BIÈRES-FRITES-GENIÈVRES

Bar Restaurant

Cantaloupe
Bar & Grill

COQ d'ARGENT

the player

BISTR②T

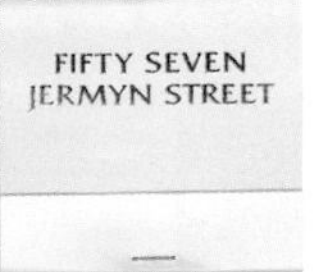
FIFTY SEVEN
JERMYN STREET

JACS BAR
AND GALLERY

R·K·STANLEYS

Bartok

BEACH
BLANKET
BABYLON

CIRCUS
Restaurant & Bar

10
ROOM

the crescent